D1570483

MARAUDERS OF THE INDIAN NATIONS

THE BILL COOK GANG AND CHEROKEE BILL

MARAUDERS OF THE INDIAN NATIONS

THE BILL COOK GANG AND CHEROKEE BILL

BY GLENN SHIRLEY

Barbed Wire Press

P.O. Box 2107, Stillwater, OK 74076

A Western Publications Company

Library of Congress Cataloging-in-Publication Data

Shirley, Glenn
    Marauders of the Indian Nations : the Bill Cook gang and Cherokee Bill / by Glenn Shirley. — 1st ed.
    p.   c.m.
    Includes bibliographical references and index.
    ISBN 0-935269-15-0
    1. Cook, Bill. 2. Cherokee Bill, 1876-1896. 3. Outlaws—Indian Territory—Biography. 4. Outlaws—
Oklahoma—Biography. 5. Frontier and pioneer life—Indian Territory. 6. Frontier and pioneer life—
Oklahoma. I. Title.
F698.C66S55 1994   94-27935
976.6'04'0922—dc20   CIP

Cover and book design by Kelly A. Reed

Copyright © 1994 by Glenn Shirley
All rights reserved
Published by Barbed Wire Press, P.O. Box 2107, Stillwater, OK 74076
Manufactured in the United States of America. First Edition.

CONTENTS

PHOTOGRAPHS

MAP

PREFACE

Numerous books and historical journals have dealt at length with the outlaw gangs that infested the Oklahoma and Indian territories in the 1890s—the Dalton brothers, Bill Doolin, Zip Wyatt and Ike Black, Vic and Jim Casey, Bob and Bill Christian, Al and Frank Jennings, Nathaniel "Texas Jack" Reed, Henry Starr, and the scavengers and rapists led by Rufus Buck. The names are legion and ambrosia to the aficionado.

Little has been written about William Tuttle "Bill" Cook.

Few have ever heard of the Bill Cook Gang. The Indian Territory press called him "The Famous Outlaw." To those close to him he was an ordinary cowboy gone wrong. Newspapers from Kansas City to Texas, and east to New York, touted him as the leader of the worst band of cutthroats west of the Mississippi.

Vying for gang dominance and a notoriety even greater than Cook's was Crawford Goldsby, alias "Cherokee Bill"—a mixed-blood desperado with no compunction for shedding blood. Cook and Goldsby traveled side-by-side on the highway to damnation and continued their parallel in front-page prominence during the waning years of Judge Isaac Charles Parker's great criminal court at Fort Smith, Arkansas.

Under Cook and Goldsby rode such disreputables as Henry "Texas Jack Starr" Munson, Curtis "Curt" Dayson, Alonzo "Lon" Gordon, Jess "Buck" Snyder, Elmer "Chicken" Lucas, James "Jim" French, George Sanders, Thurman "Skeeter" Baldwin, and Sam McWilliams, alias "Verdigris Kid." From time to time they were joined by others.

From mid-1894 into early 1896—singly, in pairs, trios and sex-tets—the Cook-Goldsby bandits defied the Lighthorse (national guard) of the Cherokee and Creek nations, the Indian police of the Union Agency at Muskogee, Indian district sheriffs, and United States marshals. They plundered almost at will all towns along the St. Louis, Iron Mountain and Southern (Kansas-Arkansas Valley) Railroad north to the Kansas border, killing whenever shown resistance. The Missouri, Kansas and Texas (Katy) Railroad between Fort Gibson and Vinita, and the St. Louis and San Francisco (Frisco) Railroad from Vinita southwest to Catoosa, Red Fork and Sapulpa, likewise found it unsafe to carry valuable express matter and passengers at night and changed schedules, going through only in the daytime and then under heavy guard.

The gang became so ravenous and elusive that Washington was on the verge of sending regular army detachments to assist the Indian officers and federal marshals. The United States govern-ment, Cherokee and Creek authorities, railroads and express companies offered thousands of dollars in rewards, dead or alive, or for arrest and conviction. A portion of the gang fled across the Red River, and led Texas Rangers and county sheriffs on a des-perate chase west into New Mexico Territory.

Unwittingly, the Cook-Goldsby bandits played an important role in the struggle for Oklahoma statehood. Neighboring Kansas, Arkansas, Texas, and Missouri deducted their depreda-tions from the benefits received by maintaining United States courts to capture and convict them and concluded it was a losing business—only statehood for the Twin Territories could do away with what they termed "the home of the outlaw."

The Cook-Goldsby combination was perhaps the most vicious band of criminals that scourged the West.

Glenn Shirley
Stillwater, Oklahoma, 1994

I

Bill Cook Takes the Outlaw Trail

James Cook, the father of William Tuttle "Bill" Cook, was a Southerner from Tennessee who fought in the Civil War with the Union Army. Like many others after the war, he drifted west into Indian Territory, where he married the widow of one Mat Morton. The widow lived at Fort Gibson, had a daughter named Lou by her previous marriage, and was a quarter-blood Cherokee. Thus James Cook secured the rights of an intermarried citizen of the Cherokee Nation. The family settled four miles north of Fort Gibson on the east side of the Grand (or Neosho) River, where Bill was born on December 19, 1873. After Bill's birth, the father "sold out" and moved upriver five miles on the opposite side. There a second son, James "Jim," Jr., was born on October 16, 1877.[1]

"Six or seven months" after Jim was born, the father died. Mrs. Cook "became dissatisfied," rented the farm, sold most of the livestock, and moved to a place near Fort Smith, Arkansas. "Little did I think then that we would be hurled about the rest of our lives," Bill recalled. "We stayed in Arkansas some time, then went back to the dear old place…making our living the best we could, only four in the family [the mother, Bill, Jim and Lou], and once in a while

1

a hired man....After a while mother sold the place and moved to Fort Gibson where she could send us boys to school....We went there about one year, then moved back up on Grand river and rented a place where we lived a while....Mother married again...a half-breed Cherokee. Everything went well. Jim and I were big enough to go fishing and hunting, but we never used any guns. Mother wouldn't let us....We were as happy as larks."[2]

In the mid-1880s, the stepfather moved the family to the Hulbert area near Fourteen Mile Creek, fourteen miles west of Tahlequah on the Tahlequah-Fort Gibson road. Shortly afterwards the mother died, and the stepfather made away with all her property and deserted the children.

"A cousin [of the stepfather]," Bill remembered, "took Jim and me home with him. We stayed there a good while, and finally he took us to the orphan's school [Cherokee Orphan Asylum at Tahlequah]. We didn't stay long...didn't have an eligibility order from the board of education." Discharged in 1887, the boys returned to Fourteen Mile Creek.[3]

Stepsister Lou had married a Fort Gibson youth named Robert "Bob" Harden. Harden was employed as a cook at Halfway House—a log establishment on Fourteen Mile Creek equidistant between Tahlequah and Fort Gibson, where travelers stopped for meals, and operated by Effie Crittenden and her part-Cherokee husband, Richard "Dick" Crittenden. Jim Cook found temporary abode with the Hardens; Bill roamed about until he became dissatisfied with the Cherokee country and went to the Creek Nation. He was then fourteen, his brother nearly eleven.

Bill found employment on the ranch of F.W. Sawyer. "I worked there until I made a pretty good 'corn hand.' I then went to the F S Ranch [of Captain Frederick Severs] where I did nothing for two years but work cattle with a pretty rowdy set of boys, and soon learned to be a rowdy myself. I had learned everything about cowpunching then except drinking and gambling, and that I soon caught onto, not having anyone to stop or tell me I was doing wrong; instead, the boys insisted I would never make a cowpuncher until I knew how to drink and play cards. In the spring of '91 I quit the F S and went to work for the Spike S Ranch [southeast of Sapulpa]. I was with a rowdier set of boys than ever before, but they were good jolly fellows. I blowed everything I made for whiskey; then I went to selling whiskey [to the Indians]....

"In 1892 I heard the U.S. marshals had a warrant for me and I went to New Mexico territory near Puerto de Luna [northwest of Fort Sumner] and punched cattle for a man named Page—the A-Cross brand, I think it was."[4]

Bill returned to Indian Territory in 1893. "By that time I had learned to be a little tough. I looked up several of the old boys I used to know. Some were living peaceably and some were on the lookout. My best friend, Jim Turner, was on the dodge, so I got in with him, but soon told him we were going to get in so far we couldn't turn back. He went to Texas and I stayed in the Territory. I was in love with a girl in that country...."[5]

The girl was pretty Martha Pittman, who lived with her parents near Tahlequah. Bill had met her after his discharge from the Cherokee Orphanage when both were fourteen. She loved him "devoutedly," but her father objected to the match because of Bill's wild ways. So they had kept their plans secret.[6]

"I still intended to marry and settle down," Bill related. "I made up my mind to plead guilty for selling whiskey and get out as easy as I could...." He was sentenced to forty days in the United States jail at Fort Smith.[7]

After serving his time, Bill again approached Pittman about marrying his daughter, and was again rebuffed. "I was not fixed well enough to marry and had been in jail....To get fixed well enough and to impress Martha's parents, I got in with Deputy Sam Harris, the sorriest deputy marshal on the force. He was more like a granny woman than anything else...meaner than I am. He would swear a lie to stick a man; that is a thing I would not do....I worked with him about two months as posse but never got but $7....I quit old Sam then and made several trips with Bill Smith."[8]

William Tuttle "Bill" Cook.

Bill Cook, "The Famous Outlaw."

J.E. Kelly—founder of Kellyville on the St. Louis and San Francisco (Frisco) Railroad southwest of Sapulpa, Creek Nation— recalled that Cook came to his store in the fall of 1893 as posseman for Deputy U.S. Marshal W.C. "Bill" Smith, searching for Alonzo "Lon" Gordon on a whiskey charge. Gordon was twenty years old, a fine specimen physically, but uneducated, which Kelly thought "accounted for his criminal career." He was a member of the Gordon family on Polecat Creek south of Sapulpa, and had been a cowboy associate of Bill Cook's. Bill knew where many of his old friends were hiding, so was a valuable posseman for Smith. A few months before, Gordon had shot a hole in Smith's hat brim when the deputy tried to arrest him. Smith was "not anxious to crowd Gordon," told Cook and Kelly he "did not want to drive him into the wild bunch," and if Gordon would surrender, he would help him in his trouble.[9]

"I helped effect a meeting between Smith and Gordon that evening," Kelly said. "Smith laid off his gun and went to meet Gordon in his shirt sleeves. Smith was 'dead game'...made Gordon a proposition, which the latter accepted" and accompanied him to Fort Smith. The deputy kept his promise, and Gordon "beat the case."[10]

Bill Cook wished Alonzo well. Gordon, in turn, expressed hope that both of them were on the road to success.

Bill was now twenty, five feet ten inches tall, of stout, athletic build. He had black hair, but his full, boyish face, dark blue eyes, and ruddy complexion belied his Cherokee heritage. Smith considered him a rather pleasant fellow to be around.

Early in 1894, Jim Cook—then sixteen, a mere stripling weighing about 125 pounds—got into trouble in the Cherokee country for the unlawful entry of a store at Springfield and theft of a gold watch. He refused to say what he did with the watch, and was charged in United States commissioner court at Fort Smith. He jumped bail, and the Cherokee and federal authorities began a hunt for him.

Bill "tried to stay out of it," but his sympathies lay with his brother. He gave up his duties as Deputy Smith's posseman and joined Jim in the Creek Nation. "We were followed by a bunch of Cherokee Indians who accused us of stealing some horses, something we hadn't done...so gave them the dodge. I told Jim we should leave the country."[11]

Jim thought they should join Jim Turner in Texas or go to the ranch where Bill had worked in New Mexico. But Bill didn't want to leave Martha Pittman.

They were soon joined in camp by a boyhood acquaintance from Fort Gibson—Crawford Goldsby, alias "Cherokee Bill."

II

Cherokee Bill

Crawford Goldsby was some two years younger than Bill Cook. He was born February 8, 1876, at Fort Concho, Texas, where his father, George Goldsby, held the rank of sergeant major in D Company, Tenth United States Cavalry—part of the regular army black regiments, with white officers, authorized by Congress in 1866, which achieved an outstanding record on the western frontier as "Buffalo Soldiers." George Goldsby was of Mexican extraction,[1] mixed with white and Sioux. Crawford's mother's maiden name was Ellen Beck; she was half black, one-fourth white, and one-fourth Cherokee. Though Crawford's complexion was light copper, his features were distinctly Negroid, including a broad and flat nose, everted lips, and crisp black hair. But he took most pride in the Cherokee side of his ancestry.[2]

Ellen Beck was eight years old when she came to Indian Territory with the Cherokees over the Trail of Tears. She had been a slave in her father's house until nine years old. After her parents died, her father's people had taken her in, taught her to read and write, and given her a job as bookkeeper in a sawmill they operated at Fort Gibson. There she met George Goldsby, who was stationed at Fort Gibson with a United States infantry company during the Civil War.

There were two classes of black people in Indian Territory—
"state Negroes" who voluntarily emigrated from the States, and
"freedmen" who were formerly slaves of the Indians. When slavery
was abolished, the government compelled the Indians to divide
their lands with the freedmen. In the Cherokee Nation, each
freedman was given forty acres; the amount varied in other tribes.
Ellen Beck was duly enrolled as a member of the Cherokee Nation
as a "three-blood," a term used to refer to a person of mixed
white, Indian, and black descent. She took an acreage near the
old road to the Fort Gibson Military Reservation cemetery, but
made no immediate use of it. She married George Goldsby sometime after his release from the infantry or his enlistment as a private in the Tenth Cavalry in 1867, and followed him to Texas.[3]

Fort Concho, in present Tom Green County, was the center of
a chain of military posts designed to protect settlers in West Texas
from hostile Indians. It had been established in December 1867
and named after the North Concho and main Concho rivers,
which joined at this point. Almost in its final state when Crawford
Goldsby was born, it consisted of quarters for eight companies,
nine buildings for officers' quarters, a hospital, guardhouse, two
storehouses, seven corrals with stables inside, magazine, and work-
shops. All buildings were of sandstone from nearby quarries, most
with stone floors, and pecan woodwork. Quartermaster's and sub-
sistence stores were furnished by wagon from the nearest depot at
San Antonio, 215 miles away. Communications were by military
telegraph via Denison, Texas, and by stage.[4]

In 1870, Bart DeWitt, of San Antonio, had established a trading
post on the mesquite-dotted flat across the North Concho. Other
traders came, and a collection of *jacales*, adobe houses, saloons and
miserable lodging places of camp followers sprang up around
them. The town was first named Santa Angela in honor of DeWitt's
sister-in-law, a Mexican nun, later anglicized to St. Angela, San
Angela, and finally San Angelo, when the government established
a post office and objected to the masculine "San" with the femi-

nine "Angela." St. Angela became a convenient point for the ranches extending westward to the Pecos River, the southern center of the buffalo hide trade, and the main troublemaker for the army post. Cowboys, buffalo hunters, freighters, and some of the worst sporting characters in Texas frequented the town. Periodically the army had to clear out the riffraff doing business in shanties along the river.[5]

A racial problem that developed between the black troopers and the cowboys, freighters, and buffalo hunters added to the trouble. Through a feeling of loyalty and cooperation to preserve the peace, the troopers often took up the white people's personal quarrels, which the cowboys, freighters and hunters considered an affront to their pride, dignity, and taste. The admixture of black soldiers in St. Angela's dives, and their own drunkenness, lewdness, and imprudence, further inflamed passions made volatile by liquor. The organization of Tom Green County in 1874 and the administration of civil law curbed some of these activities. After Colonel Benjamin H. Grierson took command of the post and put a damper on Angela's dives, the resentment flamed anew. The Buffalo Soldiers were referred to as "Grierson's brunettes."[6]

Captain John S. Sparks, who came to assist with his company of Texas Rangers in the fall of 1877, only fueled matters. His men, weary from an expedition into the buffalo range, went to Sarge Nasworthy's saloon for drinks and social diversion. Finding several troopers waltzing around with the Mexican girls, they broke up the dance and pistol-whipped the soldiers. Colonel Grierson called on Sparks and demanded an apology. Instead, Sparks allowed that his little ranger company could whip the entire post garrison. Grierson's temper was "equal to the occasion," and Sparks failed to carry out his boast. The Rangers camped that night on the Concho a few miles from the post. Thinking they were back at Nasworthy's, a number of sore-headed troopers slipped in while the dimly lighted festivities were at their height and opened fire on the dancers, killing an innocent bystander. Captain Sparks was held responsible for the incident. He left the ranger service and was replaced by a "hotter fire-brand," Captain George W. Arrington.[7]

In February of 1878, some cowboys and hunters cut the chevrons off a Company D sergeant's blouse, ripped the stripes off his pants, and ran his fellow troopers out of Jim Morris's saloon. Upon receiving the report, Sergeant Major George Goldsby summoned half a dozen troopers with carbines and entered the side door of the saloon while the festive parties were still laughing over the sergeant's predicament. In the blazing gunfight that followed, Fred Young, a buffalo hunter, and Private John L. Brown were killed, and another trooper wounded.[8]

Captain Arrington and a party of Rangers came to the fort to arrest Goldsby for allowing the troopers to arm themselves, but Colonel Grierson challenged their authority on a federal post.[9] Meanwhile, Goldsby deserted the United States cavalry.

Desertion was the most prevalent military crime during the period; the army suffered such heavy desertion rates that some officers considered the malady incurable, and not especially serious unless the deserter happened to take government owned property with him.[10] What effort was made to apprehend Goldsby is not known.

George Goldsby also deserted his pregnant wife and his two-year-old son, Crawford. Near the turn of the century, when the Indian Wars were all but over and Goldsby had been forgotten, he was living near Cleveland, Oklahoma Territory, under the name William Scott, a prosperous farmer and respected citizen.[11] Crawford knew little about his father.

Ellen Goldsby remained at Fort Concho until Crawford's brother, Clarence, was born. Then she returned with her two boys to Fort Gibson and her job at the sawmill. Unable to look after two young children, she kept infant Clarence and placed Crawford in the care of an old black "aunty," Amanda Foster.

When Crawford was seven, his mother sent him to an Indian school at Cherokee, Kansas. The school managed to keep him only three years. Not that he was a bad boy—rather a youth whose cunning and prowess was "considerable," with a "chip-on-the-shoulder attitude," and memories of his half-black mother's experiences at Fort Concho. "Stand up for your rights; don't let anybody impose on you," was her oft-repeated counsel. At age ten he was sent to the Indian Industrial School at Carlisle, Pennsylvania.[12]

This time Crawford stayed only two years. He performed poorly in the industrial arts program, resented the military discipline and uniforms. Indian boys from all over the country went to Carlisle. Learning to read, write, and speak English was an important step in turning them into red-skinned white men. Few of Crawford's classmates were willing to join in his anti-English rebellion, and he grew openly hostile toward them. Big for his age, when a fight broke out, he was usually in the thick of it and the brains behind the fracas. Often he wandered in the woods, and when no one was around, practiced the war cry of the Eastern Cherokee.

The war cry was an eerie combination of the howl of the coyote and the high-pitched shriek of a wild turkey gobbler. Coming from a full grown Indian, to anyone within hearing, the uncanny sound was as much a threat to kill as if spoken in so many words. It first came to the attention of Judge Isaac Charles Parker's court and the people of Fort Smith when a white man under indictment for assault with intent to kill an Indian proved that he had shot in self-defense because the Indian "gobbled" at him.[13]

Crawford came home from Carlisle to find his mother remarried, to William Lynch, a black barber at Fort Gibson. He also got a stepsister. Some of her friends called her "Georgia," but the Cherokee rolls list her as "Maude." Maude had married a farmer named Mose Brown and lived near Talala, south of Nowata, on a place she had gained from her freedman status.

Crawford moved in with his brother Clarence, mother, and stepfather. Clarence was a quiet, mannerly lad, tall, slender, never married, and minded his own business.[14] Crawford, still an impressionable boy at age twelve, might too have become a useful citizen with some rigid discipline. But as is often the case in second marriages, "there seemed to be no room for the issue of the first"; Lynch showed no interest in Crawford, and the boy "fell in with first one and then another, learning new evils at every stage, including the taste for whiskey."[15]

Crawford hung around Talala and Nowata for a time, living with Maude and Mose Brown. Mose Brown disliked the boy, and allegedly mistreated him. Finally, Crawford told Brown that some day he would kill him and returned to Fort Gibson. There he stayed with a Cherokee named Bud Buffington and was employed in the store of Alex R. Matheson. Matheson remembered that "he cleaned up and swept out our store…was the best working and most honest Negro boy I knew. About the only trouble he had was a few fist fights."[16]

Others discounted Crawford as a "burly, lusty" youth, who prided himself as being "the wildest thing in pants," loved to imitate the Cherokee war cry, and was uncannily adept with a six-shooter and Winchester. People were afraid of him."[17] He never had been curbed and came to the conclusion that no one could curb him. Along the way he adoped the monicker "Cherokee Bill." He was part Cherokee, had attended the Indian school at Cherokee, Kansas, and in the Cherokee country the name "Bill" meant "wild hand," not a person to run counter to. In signing his name, he drew a picture of a cherry, a key, and a bird's bill.[18]

He was known by the monicker as early as 1890 or 1891. Frank I. Griffin, of Tahlequah, came to Indian Territory from Tennessee in 1883 and had been sharecropping among the Indians around Fort Gibson about seven years when he met a bad boy "called Cherokee Bill.…A mean negro had made Cherokee mad about something. Cherokee found the negro with some other negroes down below the depot in a ditch, shooting dice. He slipped up on them with his forty-five and peeped over into the ditch, and just as the negro shot his dice and said, 'go get the money,' Bill shot him in the mouth. It almost killed him…so Bill was scouting all down the river bottoms." Griffin was plowing his corn field. When he got to the end of the row, the youth was sitting on the fence, and laughed and joked with him about the affair.[19]

Crawford Goldsby, alias "Cherokee Bill."

Afterwards, Crawford scouted over into the vast grazing and farming country between the Verdigris and Arkansas rivers and along the Cherokee-Creek nation border.

The Frisco railroad had been completed through the country in the mid-1880s, and was kept busy hauling great loads of cattle from that part of Indian Territory and of Texas cattle driven to the new railheads for shipment to St. Louis markets. Dinky passenger coaches bobbed along behind the cattle trains. Catoosa, Tulsa, and Red Fork were the towns in the center of these big pastures, with stockyards, loading pens, and depots.[20]

Catoosa was the "most rip-snortin', wide-open town" of the three. Whiskey, though prohibited in Indian Territory, could be had day or night, and a fight could be had by anyone feeling the urge. Scores of bullet holes in the buildings evidenced the many brawls that took place. When residents saw the cowboys galloping in from the ranches or racing up town after their work at the loading pens, they lamented, "Here comes hell on the hoof!" Even the quiet little stream running by the town's front door took on the name Spunky Creek. The bottoms of the Verdigris and its Hominy and Bird creek tributaries running out of the Osage reservation to the northwest, provided excellent hiding for outlaws and bootleggers. The big general store of Reynolds & Company was the main trading place for ranchers and farmers from miles around. They had no bank or other place to deposit their money, and the store kept large amounts of cash in its safe. Colonel Sam Irwin, a widower for some years with two daughters away to school, was the store manager, also bookkeeper for the J.M. Daugherty cattle operations in that country. In both positions his services were valued highly. He lived in the office at the back of the store, kept a gun handy, and vowed that anyone who attempted to make a haul there would easily lose his life.[21]

Goldsby spent most of 1892 around Catoosa doing odd jobs and working in a livery stable. He also made a couple of acquaintances who would stand as allies in months to come. One was Sam McWilliams, a seventeen-year-old cow thief, known as "Verdigris

Kid" because his hideouts were on the Verdigris River. The other was twenty-five-year-old Thurman Baldwin, called "Skeeter," a name he had acquired on the occasion of a horse race. Baldwin was of small, slender build and the rider pitted against him scornfully remarked that he "had not agreed to ride against a mosquito."[23] A second version held that he had acquired the name from fighting those pests while hiding with McWilliams in the Verdigris bottoms.[24]

Baldwin hailed from Ohio and had worked as a cowboy near Sapulpa, before concluding that the whiskey business was more profitable. He filled Goldsby with tales of wild times on the ranches, and Goldsby decided to become a cowboy.

James W. Turley and his father had come from Pittsburg, Kansas, in 1892 and leased a farm from Jack Jackson on Bird Creek. They soon acquired more land and went into the horse and cattle business. While breaking some colts the winter of 1892–93, the father became entangled in a rope and was dragged, dislocating his wrist. "On that account," James Turley recalled, "I hired a colored boy, who came to our place looking for work. He was afoot, wearing a ragged cap, and coatless…said his name was Crawford Goldsby." In the spring of 1893, James took a job on the Halsell ranch on Bird Creek, and Goldsby stayed with his father, "doing chores for his room and board." That summer, he was "paid wages." About mid-September, "he wanted a horse and saddle to go to Fort Gibson to see his mother." The Turleys provided the saddle and Jack Jackson furnished the horse. "The boy was gone about three weeks, but came back with the horse and saddle….He was being hunted by the Cherokee authorities and deputy marshals."[25]

The clash with the law was Goldsby's first. The occasion was a harvest dance in the section of Fort Gibson known as "old town." Instead of going directly to see his mother, he had ridden to Nowata with hopes of seeing Maggie Glass, a pretty, fifteen-year-old girl with whom he was infatuated. Maggie was of black, white, and Cherokee descent. He had first met her at a dance in the home of her cousin, Isaac "Ike" Rogers, while living with Maude and Mose Brown.

Ike Rogers also was a mixture of black, Cherokee, and white blood. He sprang from a family of freedmen who allegedly had taken their name from Clement Vann Rogers, a prominent rancher and father of the later-to-become famous Will Rogers. Ike had done considerable work as a deputy under United States Marshal George J. Crump at Fort Smith, but recently had been discharged for giving aid and comfort to more territory badmen than he captured. He lived with his wife and two small sons on a farm five miles east of Nowata, in the Cooweescoowee District of the Cherokee Nation.[26]

Maggie was in love with Goldsby, but her parents detested his trouble making around Fort Gibson and, like Martha Pittman's parents in Bill Cook's case, had forbidden her to see him. Ike Rogers, too, objected to any secret meetings at his home.

At Nowata, Goldsby learned that Maggie was attending the annual harvest blowout at Fort Gibson, and he hurried there, arriving in time for the dance on Friday evening, September 29.

The affair was in a large one-roomed schoolhouse where the desks had been cleared away to make a dance floor. Some claim it was in an old stone building used for a warehouse and storage. For certain, almost the entire community was there to mix and gossip, and jump to the strident "do se do" of the caller and the music of a ragtime piano, a violin, and banjo.

Contemporary reports provide few details of the cause for an altercation that arose between Goldsby and Jake Lewis, a thirty-five-year-old man with mostly white and some black blood. Maggie Glass is not mentioned. Old-timers familiar with the incident state only that the two men "quarreled over a girl."[27]

Goldsby and Maggie were not dancing. They sat at one end of the room. His attention was all on her copper-brown cheeks, soft chin, and full lips that seemed to reflect the crimson of the dress she wore. She would glance shyly at him, and look away again, as oblivious of the girating crowd as her lover.

The music ended, the couples milled on the floor a few minutes, then the caller cried for another set. Jake Lewis, tall, wiry,

Thurman "Skeeter" Baldwin (member of the Cook gang).

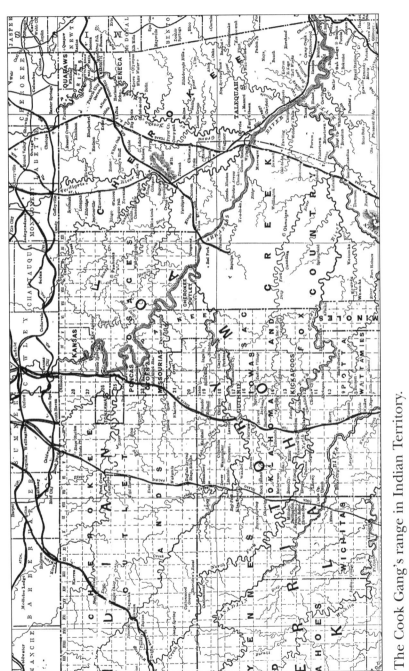

The Cook Gang's range in Indian Territory.

and more than inebriated, pushed through the crowd and asked Maggie for "a li'l dance."

She shrank back, but Lewis insisted and grabbed her shoulder. Goldsby knocked his hand away. "Leave her alone," he said. "You're a married man, and you're drunk."

That did it. Several times Lewis had fought over the implication that he drank too much. He looked over the burly youth, noted he was unarmed, and invited him outside. Goldsby accepted.

The crowd followed, forming a circle around the combatants. Goldsby was half Lewis's age, stronger and heavier, but Lewis's experience in brawls "gave him an advantage that youth could not have." Goldsby "received a brutal whipping and never again trusted himself to fists."[28]

Lewis gave him a final kick in the groin as he lay on the ground and returned to the dancehall. Some men lifted Goldsby to his feet, but he brushed them aside angrily. Maggie ran from the doorway, calling his name. Goldsby said, "I don't want to see you now—maybe later, in Nowata." Then he mounted his horse and disappeared in the night.

His fight with Jake Lewis was not over. His bravado shattered before the one he wanted most to impress, he "determined to have revenge." Lewis worked at the Charles Bowden livery barn on Garrison Hill. At sunup the next morning, sobered and the brawl of the night before all but forgotten, he entered the stable to feed and water the horses. Goldsby stepped from the manger, flourishing a .45 six-shooter. "Jake, goddam you, I've come to kill you!" he said. Lewis tried to run, and fell. Goldsby fired two bullets into his body, and Lewis lay motionless on the hay-covered floor. Thinking his enemy was dead, Goldsby ran to his horse in the woods and fled. Mrs. Bowden, startled by the shots while preparing breakfast, saw him run from the barn. "Though the Cherokee authorities put out their best efforts to catch the fugitive, his trail was lost," in the Creek Nation.[29]

When Goldsby returned the borrowed horse and saddle to the Turleys a few days later, he was accompanied by Bill and Jim Cook.

Jake Lewis did not die but was some time recovering from his wounds. On March 7, 1894, Deputy Marshal Jesse E. Jones charged in commissioners court at Fort Smith that "Crawford Goldsby, a negro, did on the 30 day of September 1893, feloniously, wilfully and maliciously commit an assault…with a pistol…upon the person of Jake Lewis, a white man, with intent him, the said Jake Lewis, to kill. Witnesses: Jake Lewis, Mrs. Chas. Bowden."[30] A federal warrant was issued the same date.

The charge made no difference to Crawford Goldsby. By that time he was riding with the Cooks and experiencing the thrill of being one of the most wanted badmen in Indian Territory.

During the spring of 1894, fifty some horses were stolen from ranches along the Verdigris and Arkansas rivers, from Catoosa to Red Fork to Fort Gibson. Posses combed the areas unsuccessfully. On June 5, Captain Severs and a posse from his F S Ranch, where Bill Cook had worked as a cowboy, came upon some men driving a small herd near Muskogee. In a hot exchange of gunfire, the rustlers escaped. Several of the horses were recovered, their theft "credited to the Cook Gang."[31]

Another rancher, G. W. Slater, discovered a large herd of horses on the Verdigris above Fort Gibson, four of which he recognized as his. He was "roping them out" when several armed men approached and told him to "leave them alone, that they were being held for Crawford Goldsby." Slater knew Goldsby's reputation, but insisted on having his horses. Finally, one of the men told him that, if he would leave, his horses would be left in the Greenleaf Hills. Slater found them there the next day.[32]

Apparently horse stealing proved too risky for the gang—or unprofitable. By Bill Cook's own statement, "It was in June…the Cherokees commenced paying out the 'Strip Money,' so Jim and I, in company with Cherokee Bill, started for Tahlequah. I told Jim when we drew our money we would leave the country."[33]

III

Battle at Halfway House

The "Strip Money" that Bill Cook referred to was $8,300,000 appropriated by Congress on March 3, 1893, to pay the Cherokee Indians for "all right, title, interest and claims which the said nation of Indians may have in and to certain lands described and specified in an agreement concluded between...duly appointed commissioners on the part of the Cherokee Indians in Indian Territory, on December 19, 1890, bounded on the west by the one hundredth degree of west longitude [Texas panhandle]; on the north by the State of Kansas; on the east by the ninety-sixth degree of west longitude [Osage reservation], and on the south by the Creek Nation, the Territory of Oklahoma [created from the opening of the Unassigned Lands in 1889 and organized May 2, 1890], and the Cheyenne and Arapaho reservation, created and defined by Executive order dated August 10, 1879; said lands being commonly known as the 'Cherokee Outlet.' Said agreement is hereby ratified."[1] The agreement, ratified by the Cherokee Nation on May 17, 1893, closed the sale of the nearly six and a half million acres to the United States.

The first $6,840,000 of the appropriation was to be distributed by E.E. Starr, treasurer of the Cherokee Nation. The first payment, for the Tahlequah and Going Snake districts, was scheduled the first two weeks in June 1894, at Tahlequah. Starr's route during the summer to make other payments would take him to Vinita, for the Delaware and Cooweescoowee districts; to Claremore, Fort Gibson, Webbers Falls, Flint, the Sequoyah courthouse, Saline courthouse east of Pryor Creek, on the Missouri, Kansas and Texas (Katy) Railroad; thence back to Tahlequah to pay citizens who failed to draw their money in their respective districts. Each Indian on the tribal roll was to receive an initial sum of $265.68. The *Daily Oklahoman* reported, "A day old baby gets as much as its father, and it is said that within the last three months 500 Cherokee babies have been born...some not yet twenty-four hours old. Families of sixteen and eighteen children are not uncommon among the Cherokee, and these will now be the plutocrats of the nation, for a family of eighteen, including the parents will receive $4,800 in round numbers as their *pro rata*."[2]

From the date of the agreement's ratification, enterprising merchants, agents, and all classes of men having goods to sell worked the Cherokee Nation assiduously, urging the Indians to buy on credit ("on the strip," as it was termed) in anticipation of the funds they would receive. Horses, cattle, everything from thread to calico to household utensils, furniture, and agriculture implements were sold, and collectors by the scores awaited the arrival of Treasurer Starr with his millions to obtain every dollar promised. Tahlequah also filled with strangers, many of them known sharpers and gamblers with hopes of a rich harvest.

The *Oklahoma Daily Press-Gazette* observed, "So far as the Indian is concerned, no tears need be shed....That individual is about as able to take care of himself and his money as any white man...he shows no trace of the hole-in-the-ground habit whatever...and usually spends it to satisfy his inordinate thirst for the cup that inebriates.

"To say that serious trouble will attend the distribution of this money is but to foreshadow facts."[3]

The last week in May, Principal Chief C.J. Harris addressed a letter to his people:

> I deem it advisable, under existing circum-
> stances, to call your attention to the attendant dan-
> gers and the melancholy aspect of the present per
> capita distribution…to the necessary caution, on
> your part, in your dealings with the hundreds of
> adventurers, sharps and tricksters now in the coun-
> try for dishonorable purposes.…
>
> I would also warn you against indulgence in any
> kind of intoxicating drinks. The too free use of
> these has been the prime cause of all the blood-
> shed in our country, and of our moral and politi-
> cal unfitness for self-government, as alleged
> against us.…
>
> The sum of money to be distributed among you is
> the largest at any time in the history of our nation,
> and may be the last. Therefore, in all earnestness
> and desire for your future welfare, permit me to
> advise you to make the best of it, by putting your
> means into good farms. Your own interest and that
> of your families demand this of you.[4]

Treasurer Starr arrived at Tahlequah the afternoon of June 2, with $1,000,000 in coin and paper money, accompanied by Captain Jess Cochrane, a former sheriff of the Cooweescoowee District, with fifty Lighthorse guards, "the surest shots in the service." As many more Cherokees, armed with six-shooters and Winchesters, were stationed about the grounds "to keep order and protect against sharks and fakirs and any attempt to rob the treasure." Despite those efforts and the admonition of Chief Harris, "much whiskey was sold at fancy prices, 'Chuck-a-luck' and other 'skin' games were run openly, and poker 'jackpots' often amounted to $1,500." Collectors got their money, by fair means or foul. Speculators took mortgages on headrights, discounting debts $10, and the treasurer's bondsmen "appealed to Chief Harris to stop this practice or they would withdraw from the treasurer's bond."[5]

Numerous assaults and other acts of violence climaxed in two deaths on Saturday, June 9. The evening stage to Fort Gibson, driven by Bill Newsome, left on schedule with seven passengers. On the seat beside him, "considerably drunk," sat a young Cherokee named Levi Sanders. About two miles out of Tahlequah, Sanders punched Newsome in the side with his pistol and ordered him to stop. The passengers were summarily lined up on the roadside. One was compelled to search the pockets of his companions. Sanders pocketed some jewelry and seventy dollars. Courtney S. Kenny, a drummer, "showed some indisposition to being robbed," and Sanders wounded him in the left lung. The terror-stricken passengers scattered, and Sanders dashed into the brush. Within a short distance, he met Milo Willey, who was herding some ponies. They exchanged shots, "one almost cutting off the side of Willey's hat." Taking Willey's horse, Sanders rode on and met Mrs. Nancy Duncan and her son, Felix, in a wagon. He commanded them to halt, supposedly to rob them, and "fired at once, striking the mother in the breast, killing her instantly." Felix seized a Winchester from the wagon and killed Sanders' horse. Sanders sprang from the dead animal and attempted to escape, but was brought down by young Duncan, who continued to fire until five bullets had riddled the Indian's body.[6]

The Muskogee *Phoenix* opined, "People who have to travel between Tahlequah and Fort Gibson have become very nervous…the roads in this part of the Cherokee Nation will be unsafe for weeks unless the Fort Smith and Cherokee courts make a special effort to clear out the lawless characters."[7] Additional officers were dispatched to the area, including a number of deputy marshals.

The Cooks and Goldsby, being on the Cherokee rolls, were entitled to $265.68 each. But the country was swarming with lawmen. Fearing arrest if they visited Tahlequah in person, they stopped at Halfway House on Fourteen Mile Creek.

Effie Crittenden was now sole proprietress. She and Dick Crittenden had separated and were on unfriendly terms. The estranged husband and his brother, E.C. "Zeke" Crittenden, lived in the Wagoner area. Both were well-known gunfighters and had served as deputy marshals before becoming too free in their use of whiskey—Harman described them as "well behaved men when sober, but quarrelsome and dangerous when in their cups."[8]

Effie always had been a friend of the Cook family. Lou's husband, Bob Harden, still worked for her, and she especially liked the Cook boys. Bill and Jim convinced Goldsby that she could be trusted and gave her written orders for their money to the Cherokee treasurer.

Treasurer Starr was to close the Tahlequah payment Saturday, June 16, before moving to Vinita. On June 15, Effie appeared at his office, drew the money, and returned to Halfway House. The Cooks and Goldsby paid her fifty dollars for her services. They intended to go to Texas or New Mexico, and Effie invited them to stay a couple of days and rest before starting their journey. Supposing that their presence at the house was unknown to the officers, they accepted.[9]

Dick Crittenden, who was one of the guards at the Tahlequah payment, learned that his estranged wife had visited the treasurer's office. Upon inquiry, he read the names on the orders she had presented and notified Ellis Rattling Gourd, chief of the Cherokee Lighthorse, that the three fugitives were very likely at Halfway House.

Chief Rattling Gourd assembled a posse at once. Most were full-blood or mixed-blood Cherokees—Bill McKee, Bill Bracket, Isaac Greece, Bob Woodall, George Parris, Nelson Hicks, Dick and Zeke Crittenden, and a Tahlequah District deputy sheriff and member of the Lighthorse, Sequoyah Houston.[10]

Rattling Gourd was the most interesting name, but Houston was the most striking of the group. He was a full-blood, tall, handsome, with direct eyes and high cheekbones. His good English and mustache gave him the air of a white man. He was thirty-two years old, the father of four young children, and hailed from Gideon (later Blue Springs), northwest of Tahlequah. He was a quick, accurate shot with both six-shooter and Winchester, and during his five years as a lawman had captured dozens of horse thieves who operated on the open ranges of the Cherokee Nation. Somber and erect—clad in a flat-brimmed hat, white shirt under a dark dress coat, and six-shooter holstered on a completely filled cartridge belt about his waist—he sat his favorite white horse and told his wife he would come home that night or as soon as his mission was accomplished.[11]

Rattling Gourd led the ten-man posse from the Tahlequah courthouse at noon, Sunday, June 17, and reached Fourteen Mile Creek at sundown.

The log structure, with a smokehouse and barn in the back, stood in a cottonwood and blackjack grove on the west bank and facing the creek. The posse planned to drop around the low ridge to the east, tie their horses in the trees after wading the shallow stream, surround the house, and surprise its occupants.[12]

Most accounts allege that "the element of surprise was diluted by the noisy approach of the officers, some of whom were under the influence of drink."[13] That seems unlikely since the officers knew the desperate character of the men they were after. In fact, Goldsby was sitting outside under a tree, enjoying the quiet June evening, when he sighted riders below the ridge and recognized Houston's white horse.

Goldsby grabbed his Winchester and dashed inside, yelling to the Cooks to prepare for battle. The posse rushed the buildings. Rattling Gourd called out, "We have you boys surrounded—you might as well give up."

Goldsby shouted back, "We will never do it, but we'll swap out with you."[14] At that moment, according to Bill Cook, "bullets began to whiz, and of course we had to fight for our lives."[15] The comic-opera finale that followed "was played in a 'wild goose chase' staged by the outlaws and swallowed by Gourd and his posse."[16]

Either Goldsby or Jim Cook, shooting from the door and side window, respectively, killed Sequoyah Houston in the first round of gunfire. Bill McKee, standing beside Houston when he fell, promptly retreated. Rattling Gourd still had the odds heavily in his favor, but he, too, withdrew when Houston fell, taking Houston's body and all the posse, except the Crittendens, with him. The Crittenden brothers had reached the smokehouse in the clearing between the house and barn. Knowing that to expose themselves meant death, they held their antagonists at bay until Goldsby and Bill Cook leaped from the doorway, firing and running to the barn for their horses. With the Crittendens thus occupied, Jim Cook began climbing out the window. "Just as he was halfway through, Dick Crittenden blasted him with a shotgun," knocking his Winchester from his hand. He fell to the ground with "two buckshot wounds in the breast, one in the hand and arm, two in the thigh, two in the groin and one in the knee." Nevertheless, he retrieved his rifle and covered Bill and Goldsby as they rode from the barn. "Jim Cook could not get his horse, so he was taken up behind his brother, and the three raced into the gathering darkness." Lou Harden had left the house shortly before Goldsby had sighted the posse. Effie Crittenden took shelter behind the kitchen stove. Bob Harden, believed to have been firing from the house with the Cooks and Goldsby when Houston was killed, was taken into custody by the Crittendens and a large posse of citizens who rode to Halfway House as soon as the news of Houston's death reached Tahlequah.[17]

It was here, supposedly, that Effie Crittenden was asked if Crawford Goldsby had been in the fight. She replied, "No, it was Cherokee Bill." Thereafter, Goldsby was known to lawmen and the press by his alias; "even his mother came to use the term in speaking of him."[18] But Goldsby was known as Cherokee Bill some time before the battle at Halfway House.

Houston had been carried about a mile away to Zack Taylor's store and laid out on the counter to await the arrival of a hack from Tahlequah. Mrs. Houston's brother, Julian Wyrick, took the body to Gideon. It was buried in the Blue Springs cemetery half a mile from the family home.

Joined by a score of Houston's angry friends and relatives, the Cherokee Lighthorse "set out to run down the Cooks and Cherokee Bill."[19] Jim Cook's condition was grave. Though closely pursued, Bill Cook insisted on getting his brother to a doctor at Fort Gibson. He and Goldsby forced a Dr. Howard to dress Jim's wounds and threatened to kill the physician if he told anyone that they had been there. With Jim riding a "borrowed" horse, they fled westward below the junction of the Arkansas and Grand rivers. Tuesday morning, June 19, they were sighted crossing the Arkansas on the lower ferry into the Creek Nation.

The Muskogee *Phoenix* of June 21 described how Jim Cook's flight ended:

> The report was brought to Muskogee....Deputy Marshal [John B.] McGill went down to the ferry to get onto their trail, and was told by someone along the road that the gang were at one Capps near the ferry....He had seen three outlaws at Capps' house, but only two leave....
>
> McGill made inquiry at Capps' and was told none of the outlaws were there....McGill took [Jim Cook's] Winchester and horse which were left and a watch which was identified as the one taken from the store at Springfield when it was robbed this spring. The Winchester was shot-marked [from Dick Crittenden's buckshot blast]. McGill found no appearance of the outlaw's presence, and left. He [Jim Cook] was there, but crawled down to the river and hid in a ravine.
>
> McGill located the others [Bill Cook and Goldsby] in Mr. Cobb's pasture [near the Capps farm], and sent to Muskogee for help....They had staked out their horses while they were concealed in the brush. McGill stole up on the horses and taking one of them rode off while the surprised

outlaws followed him with shots. [Goldsby] took
the other horse and followed him. At a farmer's
home on the Cobb place, McGill dismounted,
hitched the horse beside his own, and taking
refuge in the stable began shooting at the outlaw,
who in turn was advancing on the horses and
pumping Winchester balls into the stable at the
marshal....A lady at the farm house witnessed the
fight. She says eleven shots were fired at the marshal....She did not know how many times the marshal shot....The outlaw had gotten very near the
horses when the increased force from Muskogee
arrived, and the outlaws ran away [escaped]....

Then search began towards the river for Jim
Cook. Soon he was found and a dozen guns
dropped on him at once. He surrendered without
conflict and was brought to Muskogee and lodged
in jail.[20]

A *Phoenix* reporter who interviewed the young captive wrote:

He was lying on his cot and did not betray that he
was suffering much....His face is tanned from exposure, and he appears like a country youth who has
seen some of the world....Though he is badly shot
up, it is not thought that his wounds will be fatal or
that he will be disabled from them....He was rather
shy about talking of his exploits... answering or not
answering questions, as suited him.

He will probably be turned over to the Fort
Smith court. If there is anything left of him then, he
will probably be handed over to the Cherokees.[21]

On July 6, United States District Attorney James F. Read,
of Fort Smith, notified Chief Harris that Jim Cook's severe

wounds had delayed examination of his case, but he thought the Cherokees had enough against him in the killing of Sequoyah Houston to send him to their national prison for life. Cook was transferred to Tahlequah for trial in the tribal courts.

Bob Harden was arraigned in commissioners court at Fort Smith as an accessory in the Houston murder. At his examination hearing, defense witnesses testified that he had no connection with the Cooks, was unarmed, and took no part in the Halfway House fight. The government failed to furnish evidence to the contrary, and he was released.[22]

By July, Bill Cook and Cherokee Bill were spreading a trail across Indian Territory, fraught with robberies, stained with blood.

IV

The Reign of Terror Begins

Like many western bandits after making their first mistakes, Cook and Goldsby saw their only chance for liberty in keeping out of the hands of lawmen and living by looting and plundering. They recruited a versatile band of disreputables—Lon Gordon, Curtis "Curt" Dayson, Jess "Buck" Snyder, Elmer "Chicken" Lucas, Henry Munson, Goldsby's two Catoosa acquaintances, Skeeter Baldwin and Verdigris Kid McWilliams, George Sanders, and a young rounder from Fort Gibson named James "Jim" French.

Dayson, Snyder, and Lucas were white, in their late teens or early twenties, hell-raisers and former companions of Cook during his cowboy days. Munson was well-known on Lightning Creek southeast of Nowata. A few years previous he had been sent to the penitentiary for shooting Harry Still, a black man of some note, and traveled under the alias "Texas Jack Starr."

George Sanders was twenty-five. He began his criminal career with the robbery of U.S. Drake, at McKay, Cherokee Nation, "by holding a revolver at his baby's head and threatening to kill it if he [Drake] did not give up his money"; he was also the brother of Levi Sanders, who had robbed the Fort Gibson stage and was killed during the payment at Tahlequah.[1] Sanders hid on the

Verdigris with McWilliams and McWilliams' almost inseparable companion, Jim French.

French was older than McWilliams, small built, with a heavy mustache, prominent nose, and round, piercing black eyes. He was half Cherokee, his mother being a white woman who had died when he was a child. His father, Thomas French, was a well-to-do citizen of Fort Gibson, respected by his friends but a dangerous enemy. He operated a ferry on Grand River until his death in 1890. Meanwhile, Jim had graduated with honors from the Cherokee Male Seminary at Tahlequah, and learned the saddler's trade.[2]

"The boy inherited the nerve of his father, but failed to achieve his better traits."[3] On February 12, 1890, he was brought before United States Commissioner James Brizzolara at Fort Smith for shooting and seriously wounding Joe Ceasar, an unarmed Creek and black citizen, in an argument over a dice game.[4] Released on his own recognizance, he failed to return for a disposition of the case, and on October 15, 1892, was charged in United States Commissioner Stephen Wheeler's court at Fort Smith for "assault with intent to kill" an Indian officer who attempted to arrest him near Tahlequah.[5] He was being sought on a federal warrant issued September 13, 1893, for "robbery of U.S. mail in the Indian country [location not given],"[6] when he joined Cook and Goldsby.

The Cook-Goldsby combination began operating in pairs, trios, and sextets. From time to time others joined them. The border press soon filled its columns with hair-raising tales, fiction as well as fact, about "Cherokee Bill" and "Bill Cook, the Famous Outlaw" and referred to the combination as "The Cook Gang."

In mid-afternoon, July 2, 1894, a burly youth on a bay horse and a small built, mustached youth on a roan pony rode into the little settlement of Wetumka below the North Fork of the Canadian River in the Creek Nation. They dismounted in front of Scales' Mercantile Store. Few people were on the street. The pair casually entered the store, produced their six-shooters, and a minute later raced away across the river with a sack of money. No one tried to

Jess "Buck" Snyder (member of the Cook gang).

Elmer "Chicken" Lucas (member of the Cook gang).

stop or pursue them. The robbery was credited to Jim French and Cherokee Bill.

At ten o'clock the night of July 5, A.L. "Dick" Richards, station agent for the Kansas-Arkansas Valley railroad at Nowata, was standing on the depot platform awaiting the arrival of the train from the south, when Cherokee Bill and Henry Munson suddenly confronted him with revolvers. They ordered, "Throw up your hands!" Like Colonel Sam Irwin at Catoosa, Richards "always said that his safe would be robbed only over his dead body." He drew his own .45, and Cherokee Bill shot him in the neck. The shot aroused the town, and the desperados fled.[7]

Richard's body was laid out in the waiting room. "There was a bullet burn along the forefinger of his left hand [he was left-handed], which showed he had a bead on the robber but was perhaps a second too late to fire."[8] He left a wife and two small children. "Cherokee Bill is the fiercest of the Cook gang," bemoaned the territorial press. "Should he be killed the band would go to pieces."[9]

At nine o'clock the morning of July 6—eleven hours after the Nowata murder—six highwaymen held up the stage running between Muskogee and Fort Gibson. A mile east of the Arkansas, the bandits robbed passengers Joshua Ross, superintendent of the Cherokee Male Seminary at Tahlequah; J.W. Singleton, manager of the Phoenix Printing Company; and a drummer named Norris of their money and other valuables. "The bandits were armed with the usual Winchesters and six-shooters, and their identity was concealed [wearing masks]." However, "they doubtlessly were the Cook gang." About an hour later, the same parties held up William Drew, a prominent Cherokee, two miles on the other side of the river, and robbed him of a fine pistol and belt and eighty dollars in money. "A posse has left Muskogee in pursuit, but owing to the heavy cane brakes in the Arkansas bottom, the chances are against their capture."[10]

The Cherokee payment had closed at Vinita on June 30 and at Claremore the second week of July. It opened at Fort Gibson on July

12. The Cook gang's presence in the area caused great concern.

The Eufaula *Indian Journal* reported, "The mountains and the river bottoms offer friendly shelter to the outlaws. Travelers and country people with money about them are in a state of constant apprehension.

"Sunday night [July 8] the depot at Illinois station was held up....Monday a man from Muldrow was killed and robbed of $1,000...and within the past three weeks the depot at Fort Gibson has been twice robbed."[11]

A clash with the heavy concentration of Lighthorse guards around Fort Gibson became too risky, and the gang fled back to the Creek Nation. They had better fish to fry at Red Fork, on July 16.

Bill Cook had been tipped that a large amount of money was coming into Red Fork on the Frisco as payment for a shipment of cattle from the Spike S ranch. Shortly before train time, they captured the station agent. As the train pulled in, Munson, Baldwin, and Dayson took charge of the engine crew. Elmer Lucas—nicknamed "Chicken" that day by his companions because he had been leary of the affair—held the horses. Cook and Cherokee Bill went to the express car. When the messenger opened the door, they ordered him "to put up his hands and drag out the money."

In raising his hands, the messenger dropped his receipt book on the platform. "There is no money on the train," he told the bandits. They searched the car, taking fifteen dollars in an envelope, a box of cigars, and a jug of whiskey that had been consigned to a prominent Red Fork citizen.

The bandits took the whiskey into the passenger coach, telling everyone to be quiet and they wouldn't be harmed, then uncorked the jug and "started passing drinks around." An old man asked for a "second snort," as it was "very good whiskey to be found in Indian Territory."

The gang held the train crew nearly forty minutes before Cook finally told them to pull out for Sapulpa. The express messenger asked if he might get his receipt book from the platform, and Cook replied, "Hell yes—we don't want your old book."

After the train moved on and the bandits departed, it became known that the messenger had put the ranch money inside his book so it would be handy when the receipt was signed."[12]

Shortly after ten o'clock Monday morning, July 30, five armed men rode into Chandler, Oklahoma Territory, from the east, and dismounted at the Lincoln County Bank. Two stood guard outside with Winchesters; three rushed inside, covered President O.B. Kees and his brother, Cashier Harvey Kees, with six-shooters, and demanded that they "cash up purty damned quick." President Kees explained that the safe was time-locked and could not be opened. One robber stepped into Kees' private office, where teller Fred Hoyt lay sick. The robber ordered Hoyt "to try his hand at the safe." The .45 pointed at Hoyt's face "had not the effect of stemming his weakness," and he fell to the floor in a faint. The robbers grabbed some $200 laying on the counter and ran from the bank.

J.W. Mitchell, who was sitting in front of his barber shop across the street, had observed the two guards and five horses, and cried out, "Robbers are in town!" One of them told him to shut up; he failed to heed the warning and was shot dead on the sidewalk. Another citizen ran to the courthouse to notify Sheriff Claude Parker.

Sheriff Parker reached the scene as the robbers were mounting. Forgetting "common prudence," he "stood in the street and emptied his revolver," wounding one bandit and killing one of their horses. They returned his fire, without effect, and "rode east, the direction they came."

Parker pursued with a posse of citizens and two deputy sherriffs. A short distance northeast of Chandler, the posse met a distraught farmer who had been driving a team and wagon. The robbers had "cut one of his horses out of its harness and rode off with it."

The robbers were tracked three miles farther into some timber. "As the posse entered the trees, a bullet whistled overhead. They answered with a salvo," and found Chicken Lucas in the brush, "shot in the hip and thighs of both legs." Lucas told the posse that the others had taken his horse and left him, and were the Cook bandits. He was jailed at Chandler. Mitchell, the barber, was fifty-three years old, well-liked, and left a wife and two small children. His death incensed the townspeople, and "there was a strong move on foot to lynch the captured outlaw." The next day deputy United States marshals rushed him to the territorial jail at Guthrie.[13]

Lucas named his companions in the robbery—Bill Cook, Cherokee Bill, Lon Gordon, and Henry Munson, alias Starr—and confessed to the Red Rock train holdup. He was transferred to Fort Smith, where he recovered from his wounds and was indicted for complicity in the train robbery.

On July 31, Indian Marshal Scott Huffvine, of Kellyville, was tipped that the Chandler bandits were to rendezvous on Polecat Creek. Huffvine engaged Tiger Jack, a trailer and scout from the Euchee band of Creek Indians, to help locate the hideout.

The Egan brothers operated general merchandise stores in Tulsa, Kellyville, and Sapulpa. The Sapulpa store was managed by Bert Gray, an uncle of Clarence O. Warren. Warren clerked for Bert Gray, and recalled the Tiger Jack-Huffvine effort:

> At first, the horse tracks were visible, and they rode right along, making good time. After a few hours the trail seemed to fade out, but Tiger Jack kept riding. They were in the timber then and in the leaves no tracks could be seen at all. The marshal called halt, and said, "Tiger Jack, we've lost the trail and you don't know where you are going...." Tiger Jack replied, "Ugh! Tiger Jack know where he is going." He reached out and pulled a bunch of gray horse hair off a limb. "Bill Cook, him ride gray horse, me see gray hair all along, me on right trail." So it was....They failed to find the outlaws, but found where they had camped, so returned to Kellyvillle.[14]

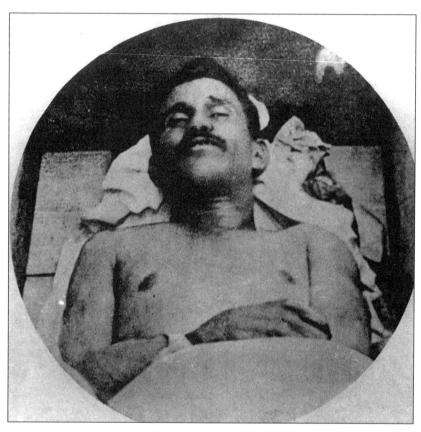

Henry Munson in death (member of the Cook gang).

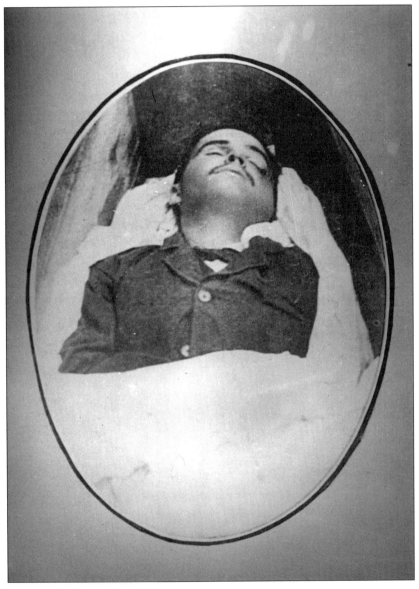

Alonzo "Lon" Gordon in death (member of the Cook gang).

Euchee Indians Jesse Allen and Thompson Pickett had been hunting the gang since the Red Fork holdup. They served in the Creek Lighthorse brigade and carried deputy marshal commissions. Learning of the Tiger Jack-Huffvine hunt, they enlisted a dozen Euchee scouts and found the gang's trail near Sapulpa. It led fourteen miles west to the home of Bill Province, Henry Munson's uncle, where the outlaws stopped for breakfast, August 2.

Province warned that "the Euchees were after them," but Cook and Cherokee Bill "didn't care a damn for all the Indians in the Territory." The outlaws had gone outside to wash up "when the Euchees rode in and opened fire." About forty shots were exchanged. When the battle ended, one Euchee had been wounded; Curtis Dayson captured; Cook, Cherokee Bill, Snyder, and Baldwin had escaped; Munson was dead, and Lon Gordon "shot through the lungs and head but lived until brought to Sapulpa, when he expired." The Euchees were "in pursuit of the escaped outlaws...determined to make it unpleasant for all law breakers who think to make this country a refuge for themselves and their associates."[15]

V

"In the Robbing Business for Keeps"

Nothing more was heard of the Cook gang until September 7, when Jim French pulled a fiasco on his own. At 2:00 A.M., he and a youth named Meigs rode to the Robert Bean home five miles south of Tahlequah and called Bean from his house, "ostensibly to rob him." Bean came out "fixed for them." He fired several shots from his Winchester, wounding Meigs in the breast, and the pair fled. "Bean came into town and notified the officers of what he had done." The would-be robbers were not apprehended.[1]

At ten o'clock the night of September 14, Cook, Cherokee Bill, Baldwin, and Snyder rode into Okmulgee. "A ball play was in progress a few miles south of town and the town was almost depopulated." The outlaws went directly to the J.A. Parkinson & Company store, demanded what cash was on hand—about $600— and "left town as unconcernedly as they came in."[2]

In the late afternoon of October 4, several riders were sighted

in the vicinity of Wagoner. "The inference was that they were robbers, and both the Arkansas Valley and Katy roads looked for a
holdup at or near that point." By nightfall, the riders had van-
ished. Unsuspecting Fort Gibson was only two hours' ride from
Wagoner. At ten o'clock, "nothing unusual was noted about the
Arkansas Valley depot…there were a few loungers…the south-
bound train from Kansas City was a quarter hour late." Apparently
deciding not to wait for the train's arrival, six masked and heavily
armed men dashed up to the station platform and dismounted.
"Three stood guard…flourishing pistols to intimidate the
loungers. The other three went inside…made the agent open the
safe and hand over about $300.…They fired forty or fifty shots as
they were leaving with their booty and completely terrified the
town." The sextet crossed the Arkansas at the ferry between Fort
Gibson and Muskogee on October 5, and the following day, on
the Muskogee-Fort Gibson road, they held up and robbed Ed
Ayers, a Cherokee, of $120. The depredations were charged to Bill
Cook, Cherokee Bill, Snyder, French, and Verdigris Kid.[3]

The gang recrossed the Arkansas, camped between the
Verdigris and Grand rivers below Gibson Station, on the Katy railroad, and the morning of October 9, again started north. Near
Wagoner, they separated, Cook and two members of the gang riding northwest along the Arkansas Valley line toward Claremore,
Cherokee Bill and the other two going north along the Katy line
toward Chouteau.

At Bull Creek, on the Valley line, the Cook contingent "lined up
the entire force of coal miners, getting about $200. They then rode
on to Inola with the intention of robbing the station and store of
H.H. Hubbard, but seeing a bunch of cowboys who had just ridden
in from a roundup, they detoured the place," passed Tiawah, and
"reached Claremore about 9 p.m." August Schaffer, the Claremore
station agent, had been notified by a local freight crew that suspicious riders were coming that way. He put all his funds on a passenger train which left the station only minutes before three armed
men approached the depot. Schaffer slipped out the back door, ran

up town and gave the alarm. Deputy Police Chief Pink Chambers was first to reach the scene. "As he entered the door, he was covered with a Winchester and compelled to donate his six-shooter, a gold watch and several dollars….The robbers then marched Chambers with them until they reached their horses…mounted and were soon lost in the darkness….A posse left Claremore in pursuit, but so far there have been no developments."[4]

The Cherokee Bill contingent fared better at Chouteau, twenty miles away. "They waited for dark, when they appeared at the M.K.&T. depot and compelled Night Operator Fultz…to give up $35 he had in his pockets." They then "assaulted" James A. Quinn, agent for the American Express Company, relieved him of a sack of gold and silver certificates, dimes, quarters, half-dollars, and silver dollars, and disappeared in the night. "Officers are out in all directions, but there is little hope of apprehending the robbers."[5]

Senator Richard A. Love, who was visiting in Wagoner, returned to Kansas City on October 10 with this commentary for a Kansas City *Times* reporter:

> I have never known such a condition as exists in Indian Territory….For daring, the Starr gang, which terrorized the Territory for many years,* can not be compared with the Cook gang which is now operating….Railway officials have given instructions to keep armed men on all their trains passing through the Territory….
>
> The gang makes no secret of its operations…ride about the country with two Winchesters strapped on each of their saddles. The people are afraid to travel, and have learned that their lives will be spared if they promptly hand over their money….

---

*The Henry Starr gang had been broken up in 1893; Starr was presently in the federal jail at Fort Smith awaiting execution, with a second appeal to the United States Supreme Court on a conviction for murder.

Deputy United States Marshal William "Bill" Smith.

> The trouble is…the Territory judicially can not be reached nearer than Fort Smith. Cliff Jackson, the United States attorney [at Muskogee], has done everything in his power and is wildly indignant.…[6]

Deputy United States Marshal Bill Smith thought something might be accomplished through Bill Cook's love for Martha Pittman. The girl, now nineteen, had not given up loving Bill, though the outlaw "had proved unworthy of her by dragging her name down with himself."[7] Her father, realizing that she intended to marry Cook anyway, finally consented.

Because Martha was a white girl, the laws prevented them from obtaining a marriage license at the Cherokee capital of Tahlequah. They applied for the license at Muskogee, and set the wedding date for late October. However, the love affair had been highly publicized, and the Lighthorse and marshals were in such hot pursuit of Cook that the wedding had been postponed. Smith and Cook had been good friends during Cook's service as his posseman. Smith picked up the license at the Muskogee courthouse, thinking that Cook might come to him to retrieve it. He hoped he could "induce the bandit leader to give up his nefarious business before it ended in his death."[8]

Still carrying the marriage license in his pocket while searching for the Claremore and Chouteau bandits, Smith was secretly approached by a Cook confederate and guided to the gang's camp. A couple of days later, the deputy passed through Muldrow en route Fort Smith, and gave the *Muldrow Register* this account of his visit:

> Cook let me come into his camp with my Winchester and pistol, in broad daylight, and I got to see most of his band.…I did not ask the names of the men I did not know, for I knew they would not tell me.…The boys shafted me a good deal about the way the marshals were after them, and I joked back. They

said they could scare a number of the marshals who had been chasing them, by simply telling them who they were....

I talked to Bill Cook a long time but couldn't do any good. He and all the gang said they would like to be out of the trouble they have brought on themselves, but it was too late...they had to live and their only way was to stick together; that "going and coming," they were "in the robbing business for keeps."[9]

Smith returned the marriage license to Muskogee, but the wedding never came off. Martha Pittman "soon learned to hate Cook as earnestly as she had ever loved him, and finally became the wife of Henry Golding, a steady-going upright citizen in the Cherokee Nation."[10]

VI

"Bill Cook to be Shot on Sight"

Shortly after 9:00 P.M., October 20, little more than a week after Deputy Smith's conference with Bill Cook in the Verdigris bottoms, the gang exceeded even their Claremore and Chouteau feats by wrecking and robbing the Missouri-Pacific Express at Coretta, a blind siding on the Katy railroad five miles south of Wagoner:

> The train was going at a speed of about twenty-five miles per hour and when within 100 feet of the switch a man sprang from behind an embankment and threw the switch for the side track. Engineer James Harris applied the air and reversed his engine, but did not have time to jump before the engine struck a string of boxcars on the siding. The robbers commenced firing at the train and engine. Two of them ran to the engine and commanded Harris and Fireman Cottrell to come down...then marched them to the baggage and express car, where by firing through the doors, they forced Messenger Ford to admit them. Meanwhile, two

49

more of the robbers had taken up positions at the
rear of the train to prevent anyone escaping through
the doors of the sleeper, two more mounted the platform between the first and second coaches, all keeping up a continual firing. During this time the two in
the express car were ransacking it. They took all the
money in the local safe and Messenger Ford's gun,
then commanded him to open the through safe. He
told them it was impossible, and after hearing his
explanation as to how it was locked they left the
express car.

The two robbers on the front platform then started
through the coach demanding money and valuables.
As they reached the rear of the coach, the two men
on that platform started through the second coach.
They were about half way through this car when a
freight train following close behind [the Express]
whistled and Bill Cook, the leader, who had all the
time remained outside issuing commands, swearing
at the passengers and shooting, called for all hands
to come out....When all were outside, they fired a last
volley at the train and disappeared in the darkness.
There were eight or ten men in the party; two of
them white, the others half breeds or negroes, possibly white men with blackened faces, otherwise they
were not disguised.[1]

The train was backed to Wagoner for assistance and to give
medical attention to the injured. Jack Mahara, advance agent for
Mahara's Minstrel Company, had been wounded in the fore-
head—he would recover, but minus a large piece of skull—and a
passenger from Van Buren, Arkansas, had a slight wound in one
cheek. Special Officers Helmick and Dickson, of the Pacific
Express, and Deputy Marshals Heck Bruner and Joe Casaver were
on the train, "but the attack was so sudden that they were covered

with Winchesters before they had time to make a move." One bandit had taken Deputy Casaver's revolver. The train was "riddled with bullets, every window being broken, the engine shot to pieces, even the steam gauge and gauge lamp being shot away." An estimated 200 shots had been fired. The mail car had not been molested. Since all agents in the Territory had been instructed to receive no money or valuables for this train, only company money remitted by local agents was carried outside the through safe, and the loss to the express company was about $500. A special train started immediately from Little Rock via Fort Smith, carrying Superintendent W.J. McKee and a squad of deputy marshals. United States Indian Agent Dew M. Wisdom, of the Union Agency at Muskogee, summoned all Lighthorse guards and agency police for duty. "The country is at last thoroughly aroused and no pains will be spared to effect the capture of the outlaws."[2]

Following Superintendent McKee's investigation, the Pacific Express announced that all money order business to and from points in Indian Territory would be suspended. The Ardmore *State Herald* of November 1 commented, "This action will doubtless serve to impress business men with the vital necessity of incorporating Indian Territory with Oklahoma, and the admission of the territory thus created as one great state."

Jim Cook languished in the Tahlequah jail pending his October 29 trial for the killing of Sequoyah Houston. Word had been received that the gang intended to liberate him, and the jail was kept under heavy guard. The attack never materialized, and Jim Cook watched for any chance to escape.

On Sunday, October 21, five guards, patently to keep an eye on him, locked a heavy trace chain around his ankle and waist and took him on a hunting trip in the woods. "At an opportune moment, Cook made a break for liberty....Though hampered by the heavy chain, he outran his guards and warded off the bullets directed at him," but was "soon overtaken."[3]

His case was reset for November 13. He was found guilty of manslaughter and sentenced to eight years in the Cherokee

National Prison.[4]

On the heels of Jim Cook's attempted escape, at seven o'clock Monday night, October 22, Cherokee Bill and three other gang members shot up the little town of Watova on the Arkansas Valley railroad, six miles south of Nowata. "At first, the citizens resisted, but were soon overawed." The gang looted the two stores and post office of Arthur E. Donaldson and Ethic Foster of $400. "They then decided to hold up the passenger train, and set the switch, as they supposed, to accomplish it...but were not onto their job." Instead of running the train onto the siding, they set the switch for the main line, and "the passenger went furiously by, throwing dust in the faces of the would-be victors."[5] Posses dispatched north from Claremore, west from Vinita, Pryor Creek, and other points on the Frisco and Katy railroads failed to intercept the robbers.

On October 23, the entire gang, again estimated at eight or ten strong, were sighted east of Grand River, above Fort Gibson. During the next three days they "conducted a thriving business" along the Fort Gibson and Tahlequah roads. "James Wood, of the Shibley-Wood Grocery Company at Van Buren, was robbed of all his money and a valuable watch near Menard. L.A. Wakefield, a drummer for the Jacob Dold Packing Company of Kansas City, and F.B. Mitting of the Daughtery-Crouch Drug Company of St. Louis, were confronted near the same place and made to fork over what money they carried." Wakefield and Mitting had taken the precaution of leaving their watches and most of their money at Fort Gibson, "for which they were roundly reprimanded by the outlaws."[6]

F.B. Morgan, a representative of the Cottage Organ Company, was "riding in the vicinity of the desperadoes' rendezvous, when two armed men, one whom he readily recognized as Cook, sprang from the trees." Cook said, "Excuse us, Mr. Morgan, but lend me a dollar; I'm dead broke." Morgan "loaned" the dollar, as well as his other valuables, drove on to Tahlequah and related his experience.[7]

Following the Pacific Express announcement suspending all

money order business, banks refused to issue drafts unless a heavy bonus was paid, and business representatives resorted to all kinds of methods to bring money out of the territory. "One traveling man brought $3,000 out sealed in a horse collar; another drummer brought out $1,500 in the bottom of a sack of oats."[8]

The night of October 26, the Cooks' stepsister, Lou, rode into Fort Gibson, "shooting into houses and defying arrest." After driving the frightened citizens off the street, she "filled the depot full of lead from her pistol, and galloped out of town in true bandit queen style."[9] It was assumed that her actions were in retaliation for Jim Cook's treatment at Tahlequah. Actually, the foray was to distract authorities from what was transpiring that same moment at Gibson Station south of Wagoner.

The town of Gibson Station was robbed in much the same fashion as the Watova holdup. "The train from Wagoner, which arrived at Fort Smith at 1 A.M., was guarded by a force of twenty-five men....The same posse guarded the westbound train leaving Fort Smith later, and were reinforced by twenty-five others at Kennetia as the railroad people were expecting a holdup at Illinois Station." The Cook gang had been sighted at the Illinois Station water tank when the eastbound train came through. "Conductor Conklin was on the lookout for a holdup at Braggs [south of Fort Gibson], but he came through all right. He reports the whole country as up in arms....Bill Cook is to be shot on sight."[10]

Sensational reports sent by correspondents to various dailies from Kansas City to Texas and east to New York claimed the robbers had left the Grand River bottoms and gone toward Okmulgee; that the Indian and federal officers were hopelessly unable to suppress them and the territory was under martial law. However, the gang was still in the Grand River bottoms, and "sent officers word where to find them and what to expect when they do." Friends of the gang "circulated reports that they had left for the Osage reservation, which succeeded in getting the Indian police, the only ones Cook is afraid of, on a long trip in that direction, leaving the coast clear for future depredations."[11]

Disgusted, General Superintendent Peck of the Arkansas Valley Railroad announced that he had a force of his own men in the field, but expected that it probably would take weeks to bring the bandits to justice, "as the men will have to first familiarize themselves with the country and people....So far as receiving help from the deputy marshals is concerned, Peck firmly believes that they would rather pursue a man with a bottle of whiskey than a gang of robbers with Winchesters."[12]

On October 31, Indian Agent Wisdom telegraphed Marshal Crump at Fort Smith that he had "reliable information" that the gang was at the mouth of Blue Creek, twelve miles north of Muskogee. He believed they intended to rob the bank. Crump telegraphed six of his deputies along the Arkansas Valley railroad to report to Muskogee at once. But the expected battle did not occur.[13]

On October 24, a grand jury at Fort Smith indicted Curtis Dayson and Elmer Lucas for the Red Fork train robbery. The jury also assuaged somewhat the grievances of businessmen in Kansas, Missouri, Texas, and Arkansas by addressing the conditions in Indian Territory and making recommendations to Washington in its report, in part, as follows:

> The causes for this state of affairs are not found in the administration of the law by the officers of this court....Its high reputation as a vigorous but fair and impartial administration of justice is too well established....For 20 years has this reputation been accumulating under the able and fearless, but patient and indefatigable labor of the judge [Parker]...until today not even the meanest criminal tried by it will question its lofty standard.
>
> In the work of the district attorney's office we find no cause to justify an assertion that the law fails of being properly and vigorously administered....The

commissioners courts labor jointly and in harmony with the district attorney and his assistants.…

If the fault for a failure to break up the crime or capture more important criminals is with any office of this court it must be the marshal's office.…But we unhesitatingly say that the fault does not lie here…that the causes for failure lie with an utter absence of a proper understanding of the situation on the part of congressional committees having appropriations for the law department of the government…a failure to provide [sufficient] fees and emoluments for the arrest and transportation of criminals.…The country is sparsely settled and the deputy cannot rely upon assistance from anyone.…The Indian people are from nature uncommunicative and averse to report and prosecute crimes. This disposition is augmented by fear of bodily injury and death at the hands of criminals.…

It seems what needs to be done is that proper and ample authority, backed with sufficient means, be given the attorney-general of the United States…to employ a necessary force and guarantee reasonable expense money and a daily compensation for all honest and necessary work done by a deputy under the authority of law…to offer rewards for the apprehension of desperate criminals.…The government is not only bound by solemn treaty with the Indian people to protect them from the depredations they now suffer, but it is in honor and in duty bound to protect the citizens and property passing through that territory.[14]

On November 10, a petit jury found Curtis Dayson guilty in the Red Fork robbery. They found Elmer Lucas guilty of complicity in the robbery, "since he only held the horses." Judge Parker sen-

tenced Dayson to fifteen years and Lucas to ten years imprison-
ment in the Detroit House of Corrections.[15]

The day of the Dayson and Lucas convictions, Lou Harden
appeared at the Tahlequah prison to visit Jim Cook and was arrested by Deputy Marshal Oliver Dobson on a warrant charging harboring the Cook bandits. "Jim, under guard, was present at the
arrest, and after tearing up the warrant which he grabbed from
Dobson's belt, he looked into the muzzle of the deputy's six-shooter,
and in a passion-weighted voice, exclaimed: 'You are taking Lou
away from me, and if I ever get free, I swear I'll kill you.'" Lou
Harden was taken to Fort Smith. En route, she told Dobson that
she had seen Bill Cook three days before, and that he would never
be taken alive.[16]

VII
Repercussions and Rewards

The grand jury report, printed in various eastern dailies, caused a stir in Washington. A committee with the auspices of Superintendent Peck of the Arkansas Valley railroad sent a dispatch to Secretary of the Interior Hoke Smith deploring conditions in the Cherokee and Creek nations: "Armed bandits are in practical control...travel through that section is confined to necessity...business houses close at sundown...express companies refuse to transact business after 9 o'clock in the morning...the Pacific Express has suspended business entirely." The committee also requested the secretary "to secure, if possible, the assistance of soldiers of the regular army."[1]

Agent Wisdom at Muskogee telegraphed Henry S. Davis, Commissioner of Indian Affairs, "My police force is not equal to the emergency and Marshal Crump at Fort Smith writes he has not money to keep marshals in the field for a campaign....I earnestly insist that the government take the matter in hand and protect its court and citizens of the United States, who are lawful residents of the Territory....The state of siege must be broken."[2] The telegram was referred to Secretary Smith.

Smith referred the dispatches to the War Department, with a

letter, stating, "In view of the obligations of the government as set forth in the treaties with the Five Civilized Tribes to protect them against domestic strife and hostile invasion, United States troops should be used to hunt down and drive out the marauders harassing those people."

Acting Secretary Doe, of the War Department, referred the letter and dispatches to General John M. Schofield, commanding the United States Army. General Schofield "looked into the matter," doubted its legality, and "returned the papers to Acting Secretary Doe."[3]

The complex relations between the military and civil branches of government caused the War Department to move with caution. "Though the government is bound by treaties to protect the Indians from domestic violence, this protection must be extended exactly as it is to the inhabitants of other territories, through the judiciary," said Doe. "The posse commitatus law prohibits the employment of troops as posses except as provided by organic law, and that law provides first for the exercise of the judicial power in quelling lawlessness, and then for the employment of troops upon application of the judicial officers, based upon their inability to enforce the processes of law."[4] To set at rest all doubts in the matter, Doe referred the application to Attorney General Richard Olney.

Attorney General Olney held that "no authority exists to use troops for the purpose of arresting the Cook gang, unless it appears that the members of the gang are intruders."* This opin-

---

*Under United States statutes, no person was permitted to reside or trade in Indian Territory without paying a tax to the tribal treasuries and obtaining a license from the superintendent of Indian Affairs, or his agents. Such a license required a penal bond not to exceed $5,000, to be secured by one or more sureties, and a new license was required every three years. Only citizens of the United States could secure a license, and foreigners were required to secure a permit from the President of the United States. Any person attempting to reside or trade without a license was classified as an "intruder," to be fined $500 and his merchandise forfeited to the government.

ion was sent to Acting Secretary Doe, thence to Secretary Smith. Smith referred the opinion to the commissioner of Indian Affairs, who reported that the Cook outlaws were not intruders— although some were freedmen, all were members of local Indian tribes. "In view of that statement," announced Smith, "the interior department will make no other request for troops."[5]

Asked by the Washington press if he had any further suggestions, Secretary Smith opened an old can of worms. "Abrogate the treaties; abolish the tribal relations; establish a territorial government and extend the jurisdiction of United States courts over the whole country," he promptly replied.

"Men who have all along been opposed to this course now see that there is no other way out of the difficulty," Smith elaborated. "I would see that the Indians were protected in all their property rights, but I would have the United States control sufficiently to rid the territory of outlaws. If a territorial Government were established, judges would be sent there to administer the laws and the governor who was appointed could see that they were enforced."

But wouldn't the whites then predominate?

"White people in the Indian territory now largely predominate, but they have no voice in the affairs of the government. It is true that in this white population there are many persons who are now causing trouble, but if the United States had complete territorial jurisdiction, they could be driven out.…All intruders now in the Indian country should be driven out."[6]

The governor of Oklahoma Territory, William C. Renfrow, supported Secretary Smith's stand on statehood for the Twin Territories. "The question has been much agitated.…Some desire statehood for Oklahoma with its present boundaries; others prefer to have the matter deferred until such time as Oklahoma and Indian territories may be admitted as one.…As separate states neither would rank among the great western states in extent or wealth. Together they would be equal to the greatest, and in my opinion, the greatest state west of the Mississippi."[7]

The *Daily Oklahoman* of October 25 observed, "No hope for the better can be indulged under present conditions. The cure is found in speedy statehood."

Metropolitan dailies in Missouri, Kansas, and Texas likewise espoused the cause.

The *St. Louis Republic* insisted, "Oklahoma must come in" and expressed specific interest in "that vast trade the new state will create."[8]

The *Fort Worth Gazette* called conditions in Indian Territory "scandalous....What a commentary on the national government that a call is made for troops to go to a section surrounded by populated districts to suppress the business of train robbing and the profession of murder. Will any intelligent person be found to advocate the continuance of such a state of things as a duty the government owes to the Indians?"[9]

The *Dallas News* and *Kansas City Times* saw in "Mr. William Cook and his school of financiers the legitimate fruit of populistic agitation and the socialistic trend of the times."[10]

To all of which the Indian Territory press took umbrage. The Ardmore *State Herald* of November 1 said, "The *News* and *Times* ought to know that questions of political economy and socialistic vagaries have no more to do with outlawry in the Territory than the man in the moon. The Cook gang are criminals from the love of adventurous crime, not from stress of pecuniary need or anarchical motives....They [the *Republic, News*, and *Times*] have selfish motives...full development of this country's great resources means millions to their wholesalers where now are only thousands."

The *South McAlester Capital* of October 31 agreed that "the majority of reports concerning the Territory is for the purpose of hastening the opening of this country to white settlement for personal gain only."

The Tahlequah *Cherokee Advocate* of November 14 made this barbed commentary: "If the business men who have established a great trade within and on the borders of the Indian nations...are to continue benefiting from said trade, [they] should stop criti-

United States Marshal George J. Crump, Western District of Arkansas.

cizing the Indian for the violence and commit funds necessary to capture the Cook bandits."

In the midst of the controversy, Attorney General Olney sent telegrams to United States District Attorney Read and Marshal Crump at Fort Smith, and to United States Attorney Jackson at Muskogee: "Put a competent force of officers in the field, offer a dead or alive reward as would result in the annihilation of the gang, and do anything else legitimately within your power to prevent the interruption of interstate commerce and the detention of the United States mails." Accordingly, Marshal Crump, listing the known Cook bandits, offered a reward of $250 "for each body delivered to me, payable on approval of the government...reward to be accepted in full of all expenses as far as the government is concerned." Five thousand posters were printed and distributed in the Cherokee and Creek nations.[11]

The Pacific Express and Arkansas Valley railroad offered $500 for the arrest and conviction of each member of the gang. Chief Harris of the Cherokees offered a reward of $500 for "the capture of Bill Cook, dead or alive." Agent Wisdom, continuing to solicit the assistance of Indian citizens heretofore reluctant to arrest, capture, or kill white men, wrote Chief Harris, "Should any Indian citizen kill an outlaw, or person supposed to be an outlaw, that Indian citizen will be protected." Chief Legus C. Perryman, of the Creeks, offered the Cherokees the privilege of pursuing the outlaws into the Creek Nation.[12]

A thorn in the bouquet was Marshal Crump's announcement that it was the sworn duty of deputy marshals to suppress outlawry within their jursidiction and, therefore, they could not receive any reward offered by the government. Neither could they receive any of the various standing rewards offered by the postmaster general for the detection, arrest, and conviction of mail robbers and post office burglars. The Eufaula *Indian Journal* of November 2 countered, "They are not going to ride out of their way to face as bold and as daring a gang as the Cooks, unless there is 'something in it.' And the law-abiding Indian citizens care more for their lives than a few paltry dollars, hence they are not going out looking for them. Then it will be seen that the notorious gang is in no danger of being captured, unless some of the marshals accidentally stumble on them and are forced to capture them in preference to being killed."

Chief Harris summoned all Lighthorse guards for duty and sent seven Cherokee policemen to aid Agent Wisdom's force at Muskogee. Superintendent Peck of the Arkansas Valley railroad took up temporary headquarters at Wagoner to supervise the movements of the company's officers in the field. An estimated 500 men in all commenced an active campaign to run down the bandits.

The Cooks, in turn, showed their defiance. A note signed "The Gang" was left fastened to a store front in Wagoner: "Chief Harris has offered a reward of $500 for Bill Cook. Come on, gentlemen, don't stand back; we are ready for you." And United States Attorney Jackson received a letter, purportedly from Cook, warning him not to allow too much pursuit or he would be sent to the place where fireworks were cheap and profuse.

VIII
Outrage at Lenapah

While the gang's philosophy until now had been "stick together," with the country plastered with reward posters and swarming with posses, they opted for less exposure than traveling in a large band. Whether for that reason, or Cherokee Bill's vying for gang dominance and a notoriety even greater than Cook's, the band split up. Skeeter Baldwin and Jess Snyder stayed with Cook. The others followed Cherokee Bill.

Also joining Cook was a small-time badman named William Farris, a companion of Cook's old friend Jim Turner before Turner fled to Texas in 1893. The evening of November 2, Cook, Baldwin, Snyder, and Farris rode to the McDermott Trading Post twenty-five miles southeast of Okmulgee.

L.H. "Mac" McDermott, an Indian, had built a long-roomed log store near his house in 1891 to supply the farming and cattle raising area above the North Canadian River. As business increased, he had added considerable merchandise, a mill, and post office, with himself as postmaster. The mail was carried by hack from Muskogee, sixty-five miles by way of Welty, a small settlement fifteen miles northwest of the McDermott post.[1]

McDermott closed his store at nightfall. A man named George

William Farris (member of the Cook gang).

Ricker was stopping overnight, and T.W. Berry, McDermott's clerk, agreed to share his sleeping quarters at the store. About eight o'clock, Ricker decided to retire. Berry remained at the house to help put down a carpet, and McDermott went to the store with Ricker. He lighted a lamp and closed the door, but did not lock it. The two men had been sitting in the store about half an hour, talking, when someone knocked. McDermott went to the door and cracked it open. Two Winchester barrels were shoved in his face. Four men pushed inside.

Cook asked, "How's your fat, Mac?"—a favorite greeting of the day. McDermott recognized him and Baldwin. He had known them before they became outlaws. He did not know Snyder and Farris, but would identify them afterwards.

Cook asked, "Where's Berry?" Informed that Berry was at the house, he told McDermott and Ricker to keep quiet and they wouldn't be hurt. "Mac, we want your money."

"I have none," McDermott replied. The robbers found only $19 in the cash drawer. They searched the mail for money and took $5.55 in post office funds. They then helped themselves to hats, suits of clothes, a large quantity of six-shooter and rifle ammunition, and several blankets. For himself, Cook took a new .38 caliber Winchester, saddle and bridle, $22 from Berry's bedroom, and Berry's cartridge belt and six-shooter.

Throughout the process, Cook "talked right smart." McDermott asked if his brother was still in the Tahlequah prison, and Cook snapped, "Hell yes—as soon as I get all the boys back together, we're going to give that place a 'round up.'" Asked why he had come this far south, he replied: "It's too damned hot in the Cherokee Nation and around Sapulpa."

The robbers took their booty to their horses, forcing McDermott and Ricker to accompany them, then Cook said: "Good night, Mac." Berry came down to the store as the robbers were departing. Detailing the event in a letter to his brother, J.D. Berry, at Fort Smith on November 4, Berry stated, "When I stepped into the place, it looked like it had been struck by a cyclone. They had mixed up all the mail in the post office. It took me half the next day to get things straightened out."[2]

The robbers crossed the river southwest into the Seminole Nation. On November 5, they were engaged by deputy marshals in a running fight, in which reportedly "two officers and one bandit were killed and two other bandits wounded."[3] On the contrary, no one was killed or wounded in the fight, and the outlaws escaped.

A few days later a German emigrant named Beckley, who was en route with his family from Wewoka to Tecumseh, Pottawatomie County, Oklahoma Territory, was "held up and robbed of all his valuables...one of the horses unhitched from his wagon and ridden off. There were four in the party. Deputy marshals are in pursuit."[4]

Meanwhile, Cherokee Bill and Verdigris Kid McWilliams attacked Lenapah. Lenapah was a whistlestop cowtown of 200 inhabitants on the Arkansas Valley railroad, within ten miles of the Kansas border and fifteen miles south of Coffeyville, where the Dalton gang had met disaster in 1892. Lenapah was of historic note as the scene of one of the Henry Starr gang's first holdups. Near there, too, Starr had killed Deputy Marshal Floyd Wilson, the crime for which he had been sentenced to hang at Fort Smith. The town's principal business was the H.C. Shufeldt & Son store, which supplied much of the northern Cooweescoowee District and handled a great deal of money. John Shufeldt, the junior member of the firm, was also postmaster.

Cherokee Bill and Verdigris Kid rode into town from the south shortly after noon Friday, November 9. They attracted little attention, except "both were strangers, a tall burly youth and one of smaller shorter size." They were "dressed like most cowboys who came to trade, were mounted on typical cowponies and carried six-shooters and Winchesters, which were no novelty in the Territory." They halted in front of the Shufeldt store and dismounted upon the large platform of the cotton wagon weighing scales, Winchesters drawn. They ordered a couple of loungers to stand to one side of the platform. McWilliams guarded them, holding the reins of both horses, his rifle cradled for quick action and adding vile oaths to emphasize that he meant business. Cherokee Bill strode inside, commanding, "Hands up!" John Shufeldt and customers Harry Clark and Levy Smith complied at once.

Clark and Smith were lined against the wall. Shufeldt was compelled to open the store's safe and sack up its contents—treasury and national bank notes, gold and silver certificates, and gold and silver coins totaling $600. Cherokee Bill also emptied the post office cash drawer, and "relieved Shufeldt of a gold watch charm and the customers of about $100."

He was bundling up some store goods that "he and the Kid might need," when McWilliams fired a volley of warning shots at several curious citizens approaching the store outside. Cherokee Bill prodded Shufeldt to the door, and was about to depart when McWilliams suggested they needed cartridges. Shufeldt told Cherokee Bill they were on a shelf in the back room of the store. "Cherokee ordered Shufeldt to get them, then changed his mind and started back himself."

A restaurant ran parallel to the store, a vacant lot separating the buildings. A side door of the store was opposite the window of the eating place, the interior of which was being redecorated by a painter and paper hanger named Ernest Melton, of Paris, Texas. When Melton heard McWilliams' shots, he rushed to the window to see what it was all about. As Cherokee Bill passed the door on his way to the back of the store, he saw Melton staring at him from the window, swore a violent oath, snapped up his Winchester and fired. "The ball struck Melton below one eye and came out the back of his head, killing him instantly."

Snatching what cartridges he could handily carry, Cherokee Bill rejoined McWilliams, who was still popping away at the town's citizens. The robbers mounted their horses. Cherokee Bill shrieked his war cry and fired a parting shot into the storefront. Then the two rode rapidly eastward, leaving the folks of Lenapah another day to remember.[5]

"A small force of armed citizens gave pursuit, but were easily outdistanced by the fast horses of the robbers." A train with several marshals and horses aboard was standing at the Wagoner station when the news was received. It immediately pulled out for Lenapah. The press labeled the robbery and murder "a senseless outrage." One report had the robbers headed for Coffeyville, where "the police department and volunteers are prepared to meet them in the way they met the Daltons two years ago." Four miles east of Lenapah, however, the robbers "turned south in the direction they had come," toward the Creek Nation.[6]

Working out of Sapulpa, Deputy Marshals Bill Smith and George Lawson learned that the fugitives had been seen twenty miles east at a popular trail crossing on the Arkansas, near the home of Charles Patton, of Wealaka. Patton knew McWilliams from his days of working cattle on the Verdigris. Promised a split of any reward money collected, he told the deputies that Cherokee Bill and Verdigris Kid were "sulking" in the hills above the river, and agreed to locate them. He found the fugitives and "stayed with them from 3 o'clock in the afternoon until 9 o'clock." As Patton would testify afterwards, "Had they imagined I was a spy, they doubtless would have added me to their list of victims." Cherokee Bill told him he had been in "a little holdup at Lenapah and had to shoot a fellow." Verdigris Kid gave Patton the gold watch charm Cherokee Bill had taken from John Shufeldt, warning him "to be careful what you do with it—it might get you into trouble." Patton met Smith and Lawson that night and "turned over the charm and the information he had gained."[7]

By that time, the outlaws had gone northwest toward Red Fork and Tulsa. But Patton also remembered that Cherokee Bill had mentioned trying to see Maggie Glass again and taking refuge at the home of Frank Daniels. Daniels was a freedman who had known him and the Cook boys around Hulbert, on Fourteen Mile Creek, and was now living on the Caney River, ten miles west of Talala.

The marshals from Wagoner station were still searching the country from Claremore to Nowata. Upon receiving Smith's dispatch, six deputies headed by Heck Thomas and Heck Bruner departed for the Caney. They arrived at the Frank Daniels place late Friday afternoon, November 16.

The structures consisted of a two-story log house, with a cellar, a barn, and several log outbuildings. Daniels, his wife, and half-brother Burl Taylor were there, but no outlaws. Thomas informed him of the posse's mission. They "didn't want the family hurt if they had to do any shooting." Daniels said: "We will just go to the cellar." The posse concealed their horses in the woods, then stationed themselves in the house and outbuildings, and waited.

Cherokee Bill, McWilliams and "another man the officers did not recognize," rode to the horse lot at dusk. As they reached the gate, one of the possemen "got excited" and fired, hitting Cherokee Bill in the leg and killing his horse. That forced the other officers to make themselves known, and "a hot exchange of lead began."

Cherokee grabbed the Winchester from his fallen mount, and "stood in the wide-open pumping shots at the posse.... McWilliams' horse was shot down....He lost his Winchester, but crawled around in the high grass until he found it, then began helping Cherokee Bill." The third outlaw rode into the timber and "never showed any more." Deputy Marshal Jim Carson "kept sticking his foot around the corner of the smokehouse as he fired," and Cherokee Bill "made a good hit....The fellow let out a cry and started hobbling toward the house." Cherokee and McWilliams then made a break for the timber, "bullets hitting the dust all around them...but made it safely." The officers were not foolhardy enough to pursue them into the brakes of the Caney. They examined the bloodstains and saddlebags on the dead horses, put the wounded Carson on his horse, and "finally rode away." Afterwards, Cherokee Bill and McWilliams "came back for their saddles and bridles, borrowed two horses from Frank Daniels, went about two miles and roped two horses from a neighbor's pasture, and brought Frank's horses back. Asked what became of their comrade, Cherokee Bill replied: 'He had a pretty good bunch of our money in his saddle bags, and we told him to beat it.'"[8]

On November 20, Deputy Bruner brought Jim Carson home to Vinita, where "he is under the care of Drs. Fortner and Bagby....The Winchester ball had crashed through his foot below the ankle, which will probably necessitate amputation of that member."[9] Deputy Thomas arrived at Fort Smith on a local and put up at one of the hotels.

"'I have just come in from the brush and don't know anything,' he told a *News-Record* reporter. He is still very sore over the fight....'Just to think,' he said, 'after I had worked for weeks and spent upwards of $200 of my own money, to lose it all because they could not wait. I told them not to fire, but they did, and spoiled the game.' Who 'they' were he would not say, and changed the subject.

"The capture and breaking up of the Cook gang soon, Mr. Thomas is inclined to think probable. He says Cherokee Bill is in no shape to do anything but keep quiet and get well. The white man with him [McWilliams] is also believed to be wounded. 'They will do little damage for some time,' Mr. Thomas says."[10]

The deputy's estimate of the pair's condition proved problematical. On Sunday following the Caney fight, a prominent citizen of Claremore, who was returning from a Cherokee Council meeting at Tahlequah, unexpectedly met the outlaws between Wagoner and Inola.

"Cherokee Bill was in a talkative mood, evidently highly elated over his escape...and jokingly remarked that the marshals nearly shot his winter clothes off. He had a deep flesh wound in one thigh and only a scratch on his arm. He had bound up the wounds himself and sewed up the bullet holes in his clothes with a cord. He expressed dislike for doctors, for fear they might take advantage of his condition....His partner wore his big slouch hat well down over his eyes and kept his face averted, evidently to avoid recognition....Both were heavily armed and kept their Winchesters in readiness....

"The horses they were riding, which they stole not far from the scene of the fight, were very jaded....The man who met the bandits was very much afraid that they would suggest a horse trade, as he was driving a good team, but they did not molest him.

"They were traveling south to join others of the gang.... Cherokee Bill says that he will die with his boots on and that some of the marshals will bite the dust, too, when he does."[11]

IX

Texas Rangers Take a Hand

Depressed by the McDermott robbery, the outrage at Lenapah and the posse's defeat on the Caney, Agent Wisdom again appealed to the commissioner of Indian Affairs: "Will not the government send the military to stop the reign of outlawry which has practically silenced the courts and subverted all law and order? Delays add to the complications. Newspaper reports of conditions in the Territory are not colored. They do not tell half the truth. I ask you to show this dispatch to President Cleveland and tell him I vouch for its accuracy."[1]

More than 5,000 citizens of Indian Territory also sent petitions to President Grover Cleveland asking for protection. These "found lodgment" in the Department of Justice, with "not a word" from Attorney General Olney. Department of the Interior officials considered the petitions "a renewal and formidable attempt to induce congress to destroy the autonomy of the Indian territory so that the country may be settled by white people." Missouri and Kansas newspapers countered, "The Dalton and Starr gangs were no sooner disposed of than Cook appeared. The conditions which foster and breed outlawry are still there, and will remain so as the influence of the white man is excluded." The Arkansas press

complained, "Marshal Crump and his men seem powerless to
check the bandits." The deputy marshals, as a corps, replied, "We
never would or could receive a penny of the reward offered by the
government…but have been riding day and night paying our own
expenses.…Let the farmer, merchant and other people in the
neighborhoods give the deputy marshal the true information
asked for and we will soon have the Cook gang where they will not
molest the law-abiding citizen."[2]

This educed one significant action. The citizens of Muskogee
posted a $1,500 reward for the arrest of Cook, Baldwin,
McWilliams, French, and Cherokee Bill, "to supplement rewards
which the express companies have been induced to offer."[3]

It "put the marshals upon their mettle," but heightened the
defiance of the Cook gang and the ire of their sympathizers.
Rumor spread that the Bill Cook and Cherokee Bill contingents
had rejoined on the Verdigris and were preparing to attack
Muskogee. "A large force of marshals left to surround the outlaws," but were "not heard from." Creek Lighthorse moved in for
a fight, but "in fear of running out of ammunition…dispatched
Sheriff John Brown to this city for a full supply."[4]

No outlaws were found, but the rumor of an attack persisted.

Word that Jim French, "the daredevil of the lot," had put up in
a Muskogee dive as a "spotter" caused the "wildest uproar."
Citizens came from every part of town armed with revolvers, shot-
guns and Winchesters. Deputy Marshal Tom Cordey and a ten-
man posse descended on the dives, searching "every room and
outhouse." But French had disappeared. He was traced to the
river, and "his course there lost at dusk." A rider believed to be
Cherokee Bill was sighted six miles north of Muskogee, but he,
too, disappeared. "No harm came to the town."[5]

Another report had the gang—"thirteen heavily armed men in
all"—some seventy miles north near Afton on the Frisco Railroad,
heading toward Chetopa, Kansas. This caused Adjutant General
Davis at Topeka "to ship ten stands of arms to Chetopa to be used
by the Labette County Protective Association in defending life

and property in that section against threatened raids from the border outlaws." The citizens in adjoining Cherokee County also "are organizing against possible invasion, and General Davis fears the military department will be unable to supply the demand for arms."[6]

The reports were soon discounted by developments in Texas.

The hunt in the Cherokee and Creek nations had grown "too damned hot," as Cook had stated during the McDermott robbery, and he had led his contingent southwest across the Red River into Clay County, Texas, to join Jim Turner and a relative, Charles Turner, with the view of robbing some trains in the Lone Star State. On November 14, this party of six were observed camped at a vacant farm house twelve miles south of Bellevue by rancher George Leftrick. Leftrick telegraphed his suspicions to Sergeant W.J.L. "John L." Sullivan of Company B, Texas Rangers, at Amarillo.

Sergeant Sullivan had just returned from an unsuccessful eighteen-day search on the Brazos River and in the Palo Pinto mountains for four men who had held up a Texas & Pacific train east of Gordon, in Palo Pinto County. Believing the men Leftrick saw to be the robbers, Sullivan summoned Rangers W.J. McCauley, Jim Wise, Doc Neeley, Jack Howell, and Bob McClure. The party boarded a special on the Fort Worth & Denver Railroad with their saddles, and left the train three miles south of Bellevue, where Leftrick met them with horses and guided them toward the farm-house at a gallop.

As they neared their destination, a picket on horseback spotted them from a distance and raced to warn his associates. The Rangers cut a barbed wire fence, crossed a pasture and overtook him after a half-mile chase. The man was handcuffed, taken within two hundred yards of the house, and left in custody of Doc Neeley. Sullivan and the other Rangers charged the shacklike structure.

The occupants opened fire through the cracks in the walls. Sullivan and McCauley answered in kind from the shelter of an

Sergeant W.J.L. "John L." Sullivan, Company B, Frontier Batallion, Texas Rangers.

old wagon a few steps from the front door. Wise, Howell, and McClure fired from behind a dugout at the back of the house.

Then all was quiet. Whether the occupants of the shack were alive or dead, the Rangers did not know.

"We have to get them," Sullivan said, "and there is only one way." He broke down the door, and he and McCauley sprang inside.

The place was empty. A ladder led through a small opening in the plank ceiling to the loft. Sullivan stepped to the ladder, Winchester ready, and shouted up through the opening, "We are Texas Rangers—I want everybody up there to surrender!"

"We will never do that," a voice replied. Another voice said, 'I want to give up." And the first voice said, "If you do, I'll kill you."

"If the man wants to surrender," Sullivan shouted, "and you kill him, I'll fire the house and burn you like rats."

A moment of silence. Then the man who had offered to surrender called out, "I'm coming down."

"Let me see your hands up and your elbows first," Sullivan ordered.

The man complied. McCauley guarded him while Sullivan waited. Only two others were in the loft, and each finally surrendered in the same manner. One man's hat had been "shot through," and a bullet had "grazed the neck of the other, cutting his coat collar and shirt." The Rangers recovered four six-shooters, eight cartridge belts, 1,000 rounds of ammunition, several blankets, and six Winchesters, including the .38 carbine and new saddle and bridle stolen from McDermott's store.

The three men and the picket refused to identify themselves. They were taken to Bellevue, put on the train, and jailed at Wichita Falls.[7]

Sullivan telegraphed Marshal Crump at Fort Smith, "Have a party of four arrested at this place. Two of them answer the descriptions of Bill Cook and Skeeter Baldwin." Deputies Bill Smith and William Ellis entrained for Wichita Falls at once. On November 22, they telegraphed Crump that three of the men in custody were Skeeter Baldwin, Jess Snyder, and William Farris. The fourth man, the first to surrender at the farmhouse and mistaken for Bill Cook, was Charles Turner.[8]

The other members of the sextet, Cook and Jim Turner, had "left the camp to locate a place where they could hold up the Fort Worth & Denver train…were within half a mile of the farm house" when the Rangers attacked, and had escaped.[9] Baldwin, Snyder, Farris, and Charles Turner agreed to go to Arkansas without waiting for extradition papers.

Deputies Smith and Ellis and four Texas Rangers arrived at Fort Smith with the prisoners on November 27. A special grand jury which was in session indicted Baldwin and Snyder for the Red Fork train robbery and McDermott post office robbery, and Farris for larceny of government money in the McDermott holdup. Charles Turner was charged for "receiving stolen property by carrying off a portion of McDermott's property in his wagon," but Baldwin, Snyder, and Farris contended he was not involved, and his case was dismissed. Upon pleading guilty in United States district court November 28, Baldwin received thirty years and Snyder and Farris twenty years each in the House of Corrections at Detroit. "Snyder took his sentence unconcernedly but Farris looked as though he had gotten more than he bargained for when he went into the 'funny business.'" Baldwin, on hearing the verdict, made his now famous remark, "What a hell of a court for a man to plead guilty in." The Rangers received $850 for their capture.[10]

The .38 Winchester secured during the fight and plundered from McDermott's store was returned to McDermott by the Texas officers. Afterwards, McDermott presented it to the editors of the Fort Smith *Elevator*.[11]

The *Elevator* lauded the United States court for its "quick work," but noted that five members of the Cook gang remained to be dealt with—Bill Cook, Jim French, George Sanders, Verdigris Kid, and Cherokee Bill.

X

"Crowding Bill Cook for Notoriety"

Correspondents continued to supply eastern dailies with sensational stories of Cook gang exploits. The Indian Territory press accounts were less confusing and more certain.

On November 26, Indian Deputy Sheriffs Wyne and Carnahan learned that Jim French was in hiding eight miles north of Tahlequah. "While searching for him, he suddenly rose out of a thicket and began working his Winchester. A running fight ensued, but the officers lost him in the brush."[1]

Three days later, a party of armed men took possession of Gibson Station on the Katy railroad. The wife of the section boss "eluded their watchfulness" and notified the next station south at Wybark. "Armed men were placed on board the train…it pulled slowly by the section house where the bandits were concealed, but no attempt to hold up the train was made."[2]

Meanwhile, three bandits led by Jim French entered the Lafayette Brothers' general store at Checotah, thirty miles farther south. "The clerks and customers, numbering nine, were lined up….French commanded the cashier to open the safe, but it was time-locked." The robbers then "helped themselves to $35 in cash, blankets, bacon and groceries," and departed in a southeasterly direction.[3]

At dusk, December 17, the Checotah bandits attempted to hold up the J.R. Pearce store at nearby Texana. "A. J. and J.C. Powell, two brave young men in charge, opened fire on the robbers and drove them off....No one was wounded, although one ball passed through A.J. Powell's clothing and buried itself in the stock of his Winchester."[4]

At seven o'clock, Christmas Eve, Cherokee Bill, Jim French, George Sanders, and Verdigris Kid visited the Kansas-Arkansas Valley depot at Nowata. "Station Agent George Bristow, stepping out on the platform, found himself covered with four guns." He was prodded through the waiting room and compelled to open the safe. "The robbers got about $190." The people in the waiting room were not molested. The robbers marched Bristow outside, mounted, and rode away to the east. "It was feared that they would rob the passenger train which was due, but it pulled in safely thirty minutes later."[5]

On December 26, the stage between Tahlequah and Muskogee was held up and "all passengers were ruthlessly robbed, the ladies being even compelled to remove their shoes and turn their hose." One passenger, Mrs. D.Y. Davis, of Coalgate, "contributed $15...all she had, and upon arrival at Muskogee she was obliged to borrow money to pay her fare home." She told a reporter for the Coalgate *Independent* that "if there was any chivalry about the highwaymen, the ladies did not discover it."[6]

The stage holdup was credited to the Cook bandits, but Cherokee Bill apparently was not among them. Following the Nowata raid on Christmas Eve, he took refuge at the Brown home near Talala. Maude and Mose Brown were visiting Ellen Lynch at Fort Gibson. Cherokee Bill sent word to his stepsister that, for some reason, he needed to see her. Besides his mother, Maude had been his closest advisor. Mose Brown objected to their going home, arguing that they might be charged for aiding a federal fugitive.

According to Maude Brown Surrell (the Browns' daughter, then only nine months old), "Mother told father, 'You know that you have always mistreated Crawford and was the cause of him leaving us once….He said he would kill you some day, so you best not molest him again. I'm going alone.' Mother boarded the train for Nowata. However, father boarded the same train at another place without her knowing it.…When she arrived at Nowata, she was surprised to see him waiting on the station platform. Mother again tried to persuade father…but he was determined…and went in a livery conveyance with her to the farm. Crawford asked father why he had come, and during the altercation that followed, Crawford shot and killed my father."[7]

Maude Surrell remembered that "the sad occurrence happened in September 1894"; the correct date, however, was December 30. The Eufaula *Indian Journal* of January 14, 1895, reported that Brown was going to tell the authorities of Cherokee Bill's whereabouts.…Cherokee Bill ordered him to leave. He didn't go fast enough, and Cherokee Bill shot him seven times with his Winchester."[8] William Taylor, a long-time resident of the Cooweescoowee District and manager of the McClellan Ranch near Claremore for several years, recalled, "Cherokee was afraid Brown would 'turn him in' and shot him seven times, and every time he shot him, Brown's mouth flew open."[9]

Within hours, Talala was surrounded by manhunters, but Cherokee Bill showed his daring by remaining in the neighborhood all the following day. "He seemed anxious to crowd all the crime he could into the old year," and that evening rode north to Nowata. "About 8 o' clock, five minutes before the northbound passenger on the Kansas-Arkansas Valley road arrived, Agent Bristow was trucking some freight onto the platform when commanded to hold up his hands and get inside." Three persons in the waiting room were ordered to "keep quiet." Following the Christmas Eve raid, Bristow had sent in his resignation and balanced his books. His successor was arriving on the passenger train, and Bristow's last official act was to "turn over the contents of the safe to Cherokee Bill." The outlaw then went to the stock pens where his horse was tied, and rode off to the

Verdigris bottoms, firing his Winchester and "gobbling his war cry as he went."[10]

These new depredations labeled Cherokee Bill the most dangerous desperado ever to infest the Indian nations. The territorial press said:

> Although he is always styled a "nigger," he boasts of Mexican, Cherokee and Caucasian blood, and seems to combine all that is vicious and cunning in the four races with an utter disregard for human life. The murder of his brother-in-law illustrates his ferocious spirit and well earns him the appellation of "gorilla."…
>
> He is acknowledged to be the quickest man in the Territory with a gun. This, coupled with his distrust of everybody makes him the hardest criminal to capture and the most feared by officers.…
>
> It is known that other members of the gang are secretly afraid of him. It is believed he is now on his own, and will steer clear of them.…He is a mongrel, crowding Bill Cook for notoriety.[11]

XI

"The Greatest Outlaw of Modern Times"

Bill Cook, having flown so high and fast as the backbone of the gang, was now alighting.

He reportedly had been seriously wounded in a clash with the Texas Rangers following his escape at Bellevue and had returned to Indian Territory. "He is lying at the point of death in the fastnesses between Muskogee and Fort Gibson...." His stepsister, Lou, her harboring case having been dismissed at Fort Smith, "has reached there and is nursing him. The deputy marshals have traced him by castaway bloody bandages and expect trouble as Cook is in the midst of a strong force of his half-breed sympathizers."[1]

A December 26 report, however, stated that "Cook is not dying, but rapidly recovering from, a hip wound received in a battle with deputy marshals some time ago."[2] Both reports proved to be journalistic concoctions. Two days later, the *Oklahoma Daily Star* at

Oklahoma City claimed, "Bill Cook reposes in a cell in the county jail. That is what the prisoners in Sheriff C.H. DeFord's charge think and they are very excited."[3]

An investigation disclosed a hoax. A young fellow bearing the "physiognomic characteristics" of the noted desperado, who used a pair of knucks on a man in Guthrie, had been brought in by a Logan County deputy sheriff. "The deputy was so nervous that, when he unfolded the warrant to show Jailer J.H. Garver his authority, his hands trembled so that the paper was torn in two. The incident suggested to DeFord the idea of passing the man off as Cook. Accordingly the prisoner was taken into the scheme." Several others in the know were instructed how to act and talk, and "all played their parts so well that nearly every inmate of the bastille was fully convinced that the same roof that sheltered his head sheltered also that of the famous badman."[4]

In Texas, Sergeant Sullivan continued on Cook's trail. Charles Turner, while in jail at Wichita Falls, had told Sullivan, under the ranger's persuasive probing, that Cook and Jim Turner likely had gone to the home of Jim Turner's father in adjoining Jack County.

Sullivan failed to locate the fugitives in Jack County. On December 22, he received word from Sheriff J.H. Harkey of Dickens County, 150 miles west, that two suspicious characters were in his town. The descriptions he gave convinced Sullivan they were the men he wanted. By the time he reached Dickens, however, the pair had gone 125 miles south to Scurry County. With the help of a Scurry County deputy sheriff, Sullivan traced them to the Square and Compass ranch, where he learned that Turner and Cook, the latter using the name John Mayfield, had pulled stakes for Green Igold's ranch a hundred miles west, in Borden County.

Green Igold admitted the two men had been there, but had departed for points unknown. Sullivan was not entirely disappointed—he recognized and arrested an Igold cowboy named Dillard, who was wanted for shooting up the Mitchell County town of Colorado City. Dillard feared facing the Colorado City authorities and offered information on Turner and Cook in exchange for his freedom. Though leery of the ethics of the proposition, the ranger agreed to forget he had ever seen him. Dillard told him that Turner had gone to Colorado City to meet and marry his sweetheart, Zettie "Sukey" Sweezer; that Turner had a friend, Mrs. Della Harris at Roswell, New Mexico, and had told Cook to meet him and his bride at the Harris home; then they would go to Mexico. Cook, leading an extra horse, had continued west from Borden County.

Colorado City officers intercepted Turner, but he escaped. Sukey Sweezer located him afterwards, and they were married at Big Spring. More interested in Cook and the rewards for his capture, Sullivan quit Turner's trail to beat Cook to Roswell. He took the train to Pecos, thence to the end of track north of Eddy, New Mexico, and rode on to Roswell, arriving Tuesday morning, January 8.[5]

At the Chavez County courthouse, Sullivan introduced himself to Sheriff Christopher Columbus "Charley" Perry. Perry was forty years old—a spare-built man, with unusually broad shoulders, a razor-like face, and pale blue eyes that were normally mild but flashed like a revolving light when he was aroused to action. Though he had never met Sullivan, he knew his reputation as a manhunter, and appeared resentful of the ranger's presence. Sullivan presented an imposing figure—six-feet-three and weighing over 200 pounds.

Perry, too, had a reputation for getting his man—and collecting rewards, by fair means or foul. He had come from Texas to Lincoln County as a cowboy about the time Sheriff Pat Garrett was hunting down Billy the Kid. He was a first cousin to Mrs. Allen Ballard, who belonged to a well-known family of the Roswell area. The relation made his acceptance in the community more cordial than his drinking habit made it otherwise. Chavez County was formed from eastern Lincoln County in 1891. In 1891, Perry ran against William "Billy" Atkinson, Chavez County's second sheriff, and was elected by a nominal majority. He had taken office January 1, 1895—a week before Sullivan arrived at Roswell.

Sullivan explained his mission. Perry mumbled something about having heard of Bill Cook. His attitude lightened at mention of the rewards. He knew the Harris family and agreed to show Sullivan their house. The ranger waited until nightfall, "having his dinner brought to the courthouse, to keep from attracting attention." Perry took him to within half a block of the Harris home, "pointed it out to him, but would go no further." Sullivan told the sheriff to wait for him at the courthouse.[6]

A man approached as Sullivan entered the gate. Sullivan asked if Della Harris lived there, and the man replied that "she was his aunt." Sullivan said, "Tell her I wish to speak to her." The woman came to the door and invited him in, but Sullivan replied that he preferred to talk to her at the gate. He told her that he was a relative of Jim Turner's; some of their party had been captured in Texas, and he was to meet Turner and a friend named Mayfield at her home. The trusting Mrs. Harris told him, "Turner had not been there, but Mayfield had been, and that his real name was Bill Cook." Cook had arrived the day before and left that morning at sunrise, asking her "to tell Jim to meet him at a ranch, the name of which she had forgotten." It was some sixty miles west beyond the Capitan Mountains, near White Oaks. The ranger thanked her, asked that she "not mention having seen him," and said he would "start toward the mountains" at once.[7]

Wearily, Sullivan returned to the courthouse. He told Perry what he had learned, but that he had followed Cook so long that he was "completely worn out and had to have some sleep. He asked Perry "to get a buggy and a pair of the best horses he could find and be ready to go with him at daylight." Sullivan noted the sheriff's seeming lack of enthusiasm for the venture, but "being outside the State of Texas, he had to have the assistance of some New Mexico officer before he could arrest a man." When he awoke next morning, a deputy informed him that Perry "had gotten another man and left for White Oaks about midnight."[8]

That so rankled Sullivan that, despite being out of his jurisdiction, he was about to go to White Oaks alone, when he learned that a heavily armed man believed to be Jim Turner had been jailed at Eddy. Sullivan went to Eddy. The prisoner was not Turner, but a man the ranger had seen at Thurber, Texas, while searching for the Texas & Pacific train robbers in Palo Pinto County.

A man and woman fitting the descriptions of Turner and his bride had been seen at Las Cruces, 150 miles west, boarding a train for El Paso. Ranger Captain John Hughes was camped twenty miles down river at Ysleta. Thinking that the newlyweds had decided to bypass Roswell, Sullivan telegraphed Hughes to meet him in El Paso. Together they made a search of the city and across the river into Mexico without finding Turner or his bride.

Sullivan was still in El Paso when he heard the results of Sheriff Perry's expedition against Bill Cook. What Sullivan didn't know was that the man who had left Roswell with Perry was Texas Sheriff Tom D. Love, of Borden County. Sheriff Harkey had telegraphed Love that Cook and Turner had separated and Cook was believed moving in his direction." A few days later, Love learned that Cook had left Borden County, leading an extra horse, going west. He found Cook's camp on the Colorado River, and from there "followed his trail over the high prairies, dry and without roads, 500 miles into New Mexico."[9]

In the first 400 miles Cook had stopped at two ranches and a few cow camps. The description was always the same: "a man of medium height, 21 years of age, with several days growth of beard, wearing a dark flannel shirt, blue coat and vest, light striped trousers and the regulation cowboy hat and boots." At one cow camp he "gave a cowboy a lot of 38-calibre cartridges, saying he had no use for them," as he had lost his Winchester. At a place called Four Lakes, Love lost the trail, but "found where a shoe had been cast by Cook's horse and, in coming off, one nail had taken a chip out of the hoof....This fortunate accident enabled Love to follow the trail in the public roads to Roswell, where Cook left the horse with the missing shoe in a pasture at the outskirts of town, saying his name was John Williams, and he would pick up the animal the next day." Love kept a "close watch," but Cook failed to return for the horse.[10]

That night, January 8, Sheriff Love rode into Roswell and sought the assistance of Perry. Perry told him they could find Cook at White Oaks. He said nothing about Sullivan, who was sound asleep on a cot in the courthouse, and the two sheriffs left on horseback.

At daylight, Love found the familiar tracks of Cook's mount near a settlement called "The Cedars," thirty-five miles northwest of Roswell. By this time Cook had reached the Capitan Mountains, one of the roughest unbroken ranges in New Mexico, and "trailing became necessarily slow." The officers traveled 110 miles that day, "Cook going in a westerly direction." On January 11, they traveled another sixty-five miles, the trail leading toward the Bill Yates ranch near Nogal. They stopped that evening at the house of a mountaineer named Graves, a short distance from the Yates ranch, and asked to stay the night.[11]

Perry claimed that his horse was sick and needed some medicine. Graves "had no horse medicine," but sent his little boy to the Yates ranch, where "a local horse doctor named Stafford always kept such things." The boy returned with "some kind of powder," which Perry, of course, "forgot to give the horse." He learned from the boy that a stranger named Williams was at the Yates place.

Perry's horse "got worse, and Stafford was sent for." The sheriff "explained who Williams was." Stafford agreed to help capture him, 'saying that they bunked together...the man intended to leave the next morning...he would take him to the corral about daylight to help feed the horses," and "told the officers where to hide in the barn."[12]

Daybreak on January 12 found Love and Perry hidden as directed. The outlaw walked within a few feet of the officers and first knew of their presence when they covered him with Winchesters. "His hands went up promptly, but he didn't seem the least nervous." When Love ordered him to hold his hands higher, "he blandly suggested that to get them any higher he would have to climb the fence." He was not armed. "He persisted that his name was Williams, and asked what they wanted him for." Love said, "Your name is Bill Cook," and the outlaw admitted, "You have the right man." The officers found fifteen dollars in his pockets, and his six-shooter at the bunkhouse in his bed. He made Love a present of the short-barreled, bonehandled .45 Colt's, saying, "I don't suppose I will need it any more." The initials C.B. and W.T. cut into the handle, he explained, stood for Cherokee Bill and William Tuttle. "The gun was given to me by Cherokee Bill. My full name is William Tuttle Cook."[13]

The nearest telegraph office was at Fort Stanton, on the Rio Bonito. From there news of the capture was sent to Roswell and to United States Marshal Edward L. Hall, of New Mexico Territory, at Santa Fe. Perry and Love reached Roswell with their prisoner on January 13. Several other officers who had been hunting Cook arrived for the excitement, among them Sheriff Y.D. McMurray of Mitchell County, Texas. "A reporter was admitted and interviewed Cook in his cell." The outlaw had this to say: "I was on my way to Old Mexico to lead a good life.…I have not been in Indian Territory since the last of October. Jim Turner never rode with me in the Territory. We have been staying on ranches, doing nothing but keeping away from officers. I have not committed half the crimes that are charged to me…all the late newspaper yarns about me and my crowd are damned lies. I did rob the Frisco at Red Fork last July. Five other boys were with me. If indicted for that I will plead guilty."[14]

On orders of United States Marshal Hall, Perry, Love, and McMurray took Cook to Santa Fe to obtain the papers necessary for his return to Indian Territory. On January 17, the three officers entrained with their prisoner via El Paso and Fort Worth for Fort Smith, Arkansas. Sergeant Sullivan met the party at El Paso as Cook was being transferred to the train for Fort Worth. As Sheriff Perry stepped onto the depot platform, Sullivan strode up to him, his eyes flashing. "That was a dirty trick you played on me, Perry," he said. "You treated me worse than any honorable officer would treat another." Perry didn't answer, but turned back into the car where Cook sat in chains, and the furious ranger followed.

"Howdy, John L.," Cook said.

Sullivan asked, "How do you know me?" and Cook replied, "I've had you described to me often enough. In fact, I figured you would be the one to catch me. Damned if you haven't camped on my trail night and day." Perry moved on to join Love and McMurray at the end of the car. Cook, leaning forward, whispered to Sullivan, "Those men are making medicine against you. All have said they intended to beat you out of the reward." Then the outlaw chuckled, obviously amused by the Sullivan-Perry confrontation.[15]

As Perry and his men were transferring Cook to the Fort Worth train, they were surrounded by reporters. Perry readily granted an interview, emphasizing his role in the capture: "Me and my deputies [meaning Love and McMurray] were in search of horse thieves when we met and recognized Cook at first glance. Quicker than a flash we had our Winchesters up and Cook was so thoroughly surprised that he lost his nerve, and although he had two six-shooters about his waist his hands went up at my command. Handcuffs were put on...he was mounted and strapped on his own horse...thus the trip to Roswell was made, a distance of sixty-five miles." Correspondents for the Santa Fe *New Mexican*, Kansas City *Times*, and New York *Sun* praised Perry as the "most fearless officer in New Mexico," called Cook's arrest the "most interesting since the days of Billy the Kid," and expanded on the sheriff's already yellowed version of the affair.[16]

Sergeant Sullivan telegraphed three of his express detective friends at Kansas City, explaining how Perry and his men had "ruled him out" of the honor of capturing Cook and that he felt entitled to "one-fourth of the reward." Within an hour, he received a telegram stating that they "recognized his claim in full."[17]

The controversy had only begun, however.

Cook was a "tractable prisoner," and the trip continued without incident, except at Fort Worth. More than a thousand people gathered at the depot to gaze at the outlaw, and Cook remarked, "I didn't have my gun. I was going out to water my horse when they came upon me by surprise...." Sheriff Perry whisked him away from reporters.[18]

The party arrived at Fort Smith at 1:00 A.M., January 20. Notwithstanding the late hour, a large crowd was at the depot and followed the officers to the federal jail to see Cook lodged in a cell with Henry Starr. During the day, Cook held a "regular levee" at the jail. A full force of guards were kept busy managing nearly 2,000 visitors eager to get a glimpse of the man, who within six months "had risen from obscurity to notoriety as a bandit chieftain and the greatest outlaw of modern times." Most of the visitors were surprised to see an "awkward looking cowboy" rather than "a regular *brigand* such as is described in cheap novels."

"That Bill Cook?" was the most frequent response. "Why, he doesn't *look* like a badman!"[19]

Cook was sketched by a young lady artist, photographed, and interviewed by newspapermen. He appeared elated when told by one reporter that, on January 14, only a few nights before his arrival at Fort Smith, Jim French and Verdigris Kid had robbed the big F. N. Nash mercantile store at Fort Gibson of all its cash, a new suit of clothes apiece, boots, shoes, and other articles. While the holdup was in progress, the editor of the Fort Gibson *News* stepped into the store and had been relieved of what money he had in his pockets. Posses were still searching for French and the Kid in the Grand River bottoms.[20] Cook chuckled when the reporter asked him where they might be hiding.

Cook admitted only the Red Fork train robbery, and said, "Cherokee Bill, not my brother Jim, killed Sequoyah Houston. Cherokee has done most of the devilment laid on my shoulders. I didn't like scouting, and I'm glad it is over."[21]

Sheriff Love was forced to give up the outlaw's bone-handled .45 Colt's as contraband. It attracted considerable attention and was later displayed at the Dingman Mercantile Company store in Muskogee.

Perry and Love claimed the rewards. They acknowledged that, though Sullivan had spent all of three weeks tracking Cook across

West Texas, he had not been in on the actual arrest. As to this controversy, the Kansas City *Times* said, "Whenever a man undertakes to
arrest such desperados as Cook, he risks his life and should be paid
without quibbling." The Vinita *Indian Chieftain* noted, "If any reward
is ever paid for the capture of Bill, it will be done grudgingly."[22]

Sheriffs Perry, Love, and McMurray entrained for home on
January 25, granting more interviews at Dallas. What moneys were
finally paid them, or how divided, is not known. When Sergeant
Sullivan wrote *Twelve Years in the Saddle* in 1908, he had not
received a penny.

Sheriff Perry made one more trip to Fort Smith. On March
18, Jim Turner appeared with his bride at Roswell, and Perry
"effected his capture." Turner denied any "robbery of mails,
stock-stealing and even murder," for which he was supposed to
be wanted, and was not involved in the fight with the Cook gang
at Bellevue.[23] The government failed to prove otherwise. He was
arraigned in commissioners court at Muskogee on an old whiskey
charge, and freed.

Perry claimed that he had expended $1,500 of personal funds
in apprehending and transporting Cook and Turner. In the
months following, he drank more than usual. He "had a mania to
kill people that posed as bad men and killers," and in May of 1895,
well fortified with liquor, he entered the Wigwam saloon at El
Paso to kill John Wesley Hardin. Hardin declared that he was
unarmed…Perry said he would place two six-shooters on the
bar…they would step back six feet and make a run for the pistols,
and the best man would win." Hardin told him he was "three
kinds of a damn fool, and walked out on him." Perry was hauled
before a local magistrate and fined for creating a disturbance,
threatening to take a life, and assault and battery.[24]

In 1896, Perry absconded with Chaves County's tax collections
totaling $7,639.02. Roswell never saw him afterwards, nor knew
his real fate. He took a steamer to South Africa, according to one
version of his disappearance, joined the British Army, and died
violently in the Boer War.[25]

Bill Cook was indicted at Fort Smith on twelve counts of robbery. Arraigned before Judge Parker on January 22, 1895, he made little defense on ten of the counts, and pleaded guilty to the Red Fork and McDermott holdups. Parker sentenced him to forty-five years in the penitentiary at Albany, New York. Pending transfer to prison, he again saw his partner in crime, Cherokee Bill.

XII

Poker Ruse for Cherokee Bill

Marshal Crump had learned of Cherokee Bill's infatuation with Maggie Glass and his attempts to meet her at Ike Rogers' home. Too, he had been informed by Ben Vann, a black man, that shortly after the Lenapah tragedy, Cherokee had appeared at a dance at Rogers' house, and had tried to gain Rogers' good will by telling him he had not meant to kill Ernest Melton but had only shot to scare him. Still, Rogers had not permitted the outlaw to see Maggie Glass.

Crump conceived of coupling romance with strategy as a means of capture. Deputy Bill Smith—though his marriage license scheme in the case of Cook and Martha Pittman had failed—agreed that the idea might bear fruit.

Since his discharge as deputy marshal, Ike Rogers had experienced considerable difficulty in making ends meet for his family. It was believed, but not proven, that he had done favors for certain Cook gang members, who in turn had contributed to his welfare. He had visited Crump in December of 1894, asking to be reinstated in the service.

Following Cook's conviction, Crump summoned Rogers to Fort Smith. He told Rogers that he would consider a reappointment in exchange for his help in bringing Cherokee Bill to justice. Also, Rogers would share in any rewards.

Rogers consented. Maggie Glass would be celebrating her seventeenth birthday on January 29. He would invite the girl to his home, and also invite Cherokee Bill to visit. He could depend on a neighbor, Clint Scales, to assist in the capture. Crump would send Deputies Smith and George Lawson to Nowata to await the arrival of Rogers and Scales with their prisoner. He instructed Rogers to take Cherokee Bill alive, if possible, and Rogers replied, "I don't want to kill him, but I will kill him if I can't get him in any other way."[1]

Tuesday afternoon, January 29, Maggie Glass arrived at the Rogers home for supper. Clint Scales was there. Cherokee Bill had been seen near the house of a neighbor named Jackson, and Rogers sent one of his boys to tell the outlaw that Maggie wanted to see him. Cherokee arrived shortly after dark, and from that moment was on his guard, prepared to use his Winchester. Maggie also was suspicious of Rogers, and while the lovers visited briefly, she warned Cherokee to leave. The outlaw refused, stating, "If Rogers makes a play, I'll show him how long it takes to commit murder."

Rogers was just as cunning. He and Scales had hidden their weapons where they would be handy when needed. Rogers acted the part of a cordial host, invited Cherokee to stay the night, and even suggested that he put his Winchester aside. The outlaw replied, "That is something I *never* do."

Rogers then tempted him with whiskey, doctored with morphine, but Bill refused to drink. Supper time came, and after the others were seated, the outlaw took his place with his back to the wall, his Winchester across his knees.

After supper, cards were produced. Cherokee played casino with Scales while Rogers "looked for any opportunity to overpower him." But "Cherokee followed his every move." The card playing continued until four o'clock Wednesday morning, when the men retired, the outlaw and his host sleeping in the same bed. Rogers feigned sleep, waiting for the outlaw to close his eyes in slumber, but each time he moved, "Cherokee would rise in bed, his Winchester ready."

At breakfast time, "it looked as if the game would escape." Cherokee Bill spoke of telling Maggie good-bye. Rogers urged him to stay for dinner. Fearing that Maggie would take a hand if trouble began, and for the safety of his boys who knew nothing of his plans, Rogers gave the girl a dollar and sent the boys with her to Jackson's house to buy some chickens for the dinner pot. Meanwhile, he, Scales, and Cherokee Bill sat around the fireplace, talking. Finally, Cherokee Bill took some paper and tobacco from his pocket and rolled a cigarette. He had no match and stooped toward the fireplace for an ember to light it. His head turned from Rogers for a moment.

Rogers moved with the speed of a cat. He seized a heavy iron poker he had just used in punching the fire and struck the outlaw across the back of the head.

The blow would have killed an ordinary man, but it only knocked the outlaw to his knees. Rogers and Scales leaped upon him, Rogers' wife grabbed his Winchester, and the three fought on the floor fully twenty minutes before Rogers and Scales managed to secure Cherokee Bill with handcuffs. The outlaw then pleaded with them to kill him or release him. He promised them money and horses, which they refused, and he cursed them for their treachery. They bound his feet with baling wire, put him in a wagon, and with Scales beside him and Rogers on horseback, started for Nowata.

En route, Cherokee Bill again showed his tremendous strength by actually breaking his handcuffs. Scales leaped off the wagon to avoid losing his pistol, while Rogers kept the outlaw covered with his double-barreled shotgun.[2]

At Nowata, the outlaw was chained and placed in an Arkansas Valley railway cattle car. People flocked around it, staring through the boards at him as if he were a wild animal. Smith telegraphed Marshal Crump at Fort Smith, "Will be there on morning train 266 with Cherokee Bill. Did not hurt him." The news spread rapidly, and every person on Garrison Avenue was agog in disbelief.[3]

Another large crowd waited to get a glimpse of the outlaw as the train passed through Claremore. When it stopped at Wagoner, Deputy Marshals Dick and Zeke Crittenden joined Smith and Lawson as additional guards. The prisoner was brought from the car in leg irons, and the entire party photographed by Wagoner photographer E.D. MacFee.

Cherokee Bill refused to allow Ike Rogers to stand beside him, but threw his right arm about Dick Crittenden, saying, "Here is a fellow that stood up and fought me like a man [at Halfway House]; I will have my picture taken with him." In the same instant, he reached for Crittenden's revolver. Had he obtained it, as he said afterwards, some of the officers "would have worn away wooden overcoats," and Rogers "would not have reached Fort Smith to receive any of the reward."[4]

Cherokee Bill was "the most disgusted fellow that ever landed behind the bars of the U.S. jail." He told an *Elevator* reporter, "I never saw the deputy marshals while they were looking for me except when the smoke was coming out of my gun. If they will just put me back on the prairie, I can whip any ten of them in the Territory." He was "placed on the same tier with Bill Cook, where no doubt the two will have some interesting conversations during the next few days."[5]

Demonstrating how badly Cherokee Bill was feared, a leading businessman of the Cherokee Nation handed Rogers a check for fifty dollars, stating that he had not offered a reward for the outlaw "because he was afraid that robbery and violence to him would follow" and the capture "made him feel $50 easier."[6]

J.E. Kelly, of Kellyville, had known Cherokee Bill intimately before he turned bandit-killer. Kelly visited the jail, and George Lawson invited him to see the outlaw brought out of his cell to be photographed. "Bill was 'hot' and crying with madness when he appeared," Kelly related. "Lawson said, 'Bill, quit your crying; here is Kelly to see you; why don't you ask him about some of your old friends?' Bill looked up quickly...smiled through his tears and, grabbing my hand, exclaimed: 'Hello, old friend!' I thought you might see me all shot to hell, but never down here.'"[7]

The outlaw was handed a beautiful—but empty—Winchester to use in posing for the picture. Kelly continued, "His eyes snapped with the old fire....After the photographer had finished, he fondled the gun and seemed loath to give it up....Before returning it, he worked the lever and trigger until it clicked like a sewing machine. It was a wonder to all how he could shoot so fast. Bill said he knew he might not always hit the target, but he would shoot so damned fast that he would 'rattle' his antagonist 'so he could not hit me.'"[8]

The outlaw's own Winchester—"a handsome .40-82 with combination sights and comparatively new"—was later returned to the Egan Brothers store at Sapulpa, where he had purchased it and given an order on his mother in payment after killing Ernest Melton.[9]

The Vinita *Indian Chieftain* of February 7 noted that, "with Cherokee Bill knocked down with a poker and captured," only Jim French, George Sanders, and Verdigris Kid of the Cook gang were "left for seed." That same date, French fell from the gang's roster, along with a stripling cowboy he had picked up named Jess Cochran, alias Swanson. The evening was windy and bitterly cold. Snow covered the ground, more was falling, and cow town Catoosa had closed down early.

About nine o'clock, French and Cochran dismounted at the office and living quarters of Manager Sam Irwin in the rear of the Reynolds & Company general store, which French had decided was "the place most likely to contain the cash they were after." Cochran took the door that entered from the passageway separating the store and office. French stepped to the west side window. He discovered Irwin working at his desk on the far side of the

Zeke Crittenden (5), Dick Crittenden (4), Cherokee Bill, Clint Scales (2), Ike Rogers (1), and Deputy Bill Smith (8) at Wagoner, Indian Territory, January 30, 1895.

room, and was about to raise his Winchester to poke out the window pane and cover him, when he sighted Irwin's young clerk and night watchman, Tommy Wilkins, seated in a rocking chair, a double-barreled shotgun in his lap. Not waiting for French to start the action, the restless Cochran sent a rifle ball through the door, barely missing the watchman. Quick as a flash, Irwin sprang to the door, jerked it wide open, himself behind it. Wilkins' shotgun roared, and Cochran fell in the passageway with most of his upper face and the top of his head gone. French crashed the window, leveling his Winchester to kill Irwin. Wilkins swung around and emptied the other barrel of his shotgun. The charge missed French, tearing into the window frame. French's shot was true. The ball tore through Irwin's body, just below the waist, and he fell with a groan. French bounded around into the doorway. Wilkins jumped behind a heavy oak dresser in the northwest corner of the room. "Come out, God damn you," French snarled. "You killed my partner."

He took several dollars from Wilkins' pockets and fifty dollars from the desk drawer—all the cash Irwin had in the office at the time—then commanded the watchman, "Help me put Irwin on his bed—no need to hurt him any more."

The mortally wounded manager was placed on the bed in the northeast corner of the room. French did not know that Irwin kept a revolver under the pillow.

"Now, help me bring my partner out of the cold," French ordered, and Wilkins helped carry Cochran's body from the passageway onto the office floor.

Then French said, "I'm going to kill you."

Wilkins pleaded that his shotgun was empty and he had no more ammunition. But French stood his Winchester at his left side and drew his .45 Colt's. Before the outlaw could fire, Irwin, though hardly able to move, brought his revolver from under the pillow and blazed away twice in rapid succession.

Both shots struck French in the neck. The outlaw dropped his guns and reeled from the room with blood spurting from his

James "Jim" French.

wounds. He managed to mount his horse, and rode toward Spunky Creek.

Reaching an old cabin three quarters of a mile from town, French turned his horse loose, burst inside, and collapsed before the fireplace. The occupants—an Indian and his son—fled out the back door and ran toward town to give the alarm. They met Wilkins, his shotgun reloaded, and leading a posse of Catoosa citizens along the trail in the bloodstained snow.

The posse approached the cabin cautiously. There was no movement inside. Wilkins kicked open the door, saw French sprawled before the fire, and raised his shotgun to kill him. But the outlaw "already had passed into the Great Beyond"—or wherever bandit-killers go. "In dying, he had kicked one foot into the fireplace and part of his boot and half of his toes were burned away."[10]

Irwin died at ten o'clock the next morning. "During the interval that he lived, he gave directions as to his affairs...expressing the wish that he be buried at Vinita by the Masonic fraternity. His remains were shipped on the evening train....The funeral took place at the Methodist Church, the Masons conducting the services at the grave....All stores were closed in respect for his bravery."[11] He had lived up to his vow never to be robbed without a fight. The dead outlaws were shipped on the same train. "It was at first supposed that Cochran was the Verdigris Kid...but at Claremore the remains were fully identified and left there."[12] At Fort Smith, French's body "lay in an open coffin for several hours at the United States jail, where it was viewed by hundreds and satisfactorily identified." Afterwards, it was released to a relative, who took it to Fort Gibson for burial.[13]

On February 8, Cherokee Bill was indicted for the murder of Ernest Melton. He pleaded not guilty when arraigned before Judge Parker, who set his trial for the last week of February.[14] On February 14, he was indicted for the October 22, 1894, robbery of the store and post office of Donaldson and Foster at Watova,[15] and on February 15, he was indicted for the October 9, 1894,

American Express Company robbery at Chouteau.[16] On February 23, a petit jury returned guilty verdicts, and he remained in the United States jail, bail denied, sentencing in both cases pending.

Lawyer J. Warren Reed.

XIII

"I'm Not Dead Yet"

The Melton murder trial began before Judge Parker at noon, February 26. District Attorney James F. Read was determined that Cherokee Bill pay the supreme penalty for his heinous crime. But there was a thorn in the prosecutor's side: the outlaw had engaged one of the biggest charlatans of the border country, but a very successful lawyer, J. Warren Reed.

Reed was a native of West Virginia, who had come to Fort Smith by way of Ohio and California in 1886 to defend a noted case. Being attracted by the magnitude of business in the United States courts, he had settled down to permanent practice. He affected an elaborate mustache and bow tie, a cutaway ("claw-hammer") coat, a silver-headed cane, and a magnificent silk hat—considered out of place in this rough-and-tumble border city. However, he possessed something to back up his pretentious dress. He was an indefatigable worker, an eloquent speaker, and more often than not, however unscrupulously, won his point. Since 1889, Reed's defense and assistance in defense of more than 130 capital cases had resulted in reducing the grade of crime to manslaughter, reversals by the United States Supreme Court, or commutations by the President of the United States.[1]

Reed knew that Cherokee Bill's finances were limited and his chances for collecting his fees were uncertain. Yet this so-called "friend of the oppressed and downtrodden" threw his "whole soul" into the effort to save Goldsby's neck and keep himself in the limelight as "That Lawyer Who Always Wins His Cases."[2]

Reed attempted to establish an alibi. Half a dozen Goldsby acquaintances, including his brother Clarence, placed the outlaw at Fort Gibson, "at least 100 miles by country roads from Lenapah," until daylight the day before the tragedy, when "defendant started on horseback a distance of about 45 miles...to a place six miles southeast of Claremore." There, according to the deceased Jess Cochran's widow, "defendant stayed the night," and next morning, November 9, "a man whose name is to the defendant unknown [Verdigris Kid?] went horseback with defendant two miles on the road toward Tulsa, Creek Nation." Shortly after noon, "defendant came to the home of Thomas Low and his wife...8 miles west of Tulsa....Low went to Tulsa that afternoon and there learned of the said robbery and murder and returned the same afternoon and informed his family and the defendant of the news so received." Joe Roach and his wife, who lived half a mile from the Lows, stated that "defendant came from toward Tom Low's to their house and informed them of the report coming from Low....After remaining [at the Roaches] a short time, defendant started on horseback in the direction of the Hendricks home," five miles southwest. Mrs. Hendricks said "he arrived at sundown." About midnight, November 9, "defendant came to the house of John Foreman," ten miles from the Roaches, "stayed a few hours, warmed himself and started on in the night." At ten o'clock the morning of November 10, "defendant took dinner" three miles south of Red Fork with William Vance and his wife, "who had heard all about the said robbery and murder, the same having come by telegram to Red Fork."

Therefore, Reed propounded, Goldsby had been "75 miles from Lenapah, rendering it impossible that defendant could have been at the place at the time of said robbery and murder, or participated therein."[3]

Cherokee Bill did not take the stand, but a freedman from Fort Gibson, who knew both French and Cherokee Bill, testified that he had been in Lenapah at the time of the tragedy and Goldsby was not present. He identified French as Melton's killer, and thought that the man doing the shooting in front of the store was Verdigris Kid.[4] Of course, Verdigris Kid was still at large, and the deceased French was unable to refute it.

On the contrary, the Lows could not be certain of the time Cherokee Bill arrived at their home, and the prosecution brought out the "rapidity" with which members of the Cook gang traveled from place to place. During the convictions of Dayson and Lucas, "it had been testified to that after the Red Fork robbery, the gang rode sixty miles in a single night." This "tended to weaken Cherokee Bill's alibi."[5]

John Shufeldt and the store's customers "positively identified Goldsby as the man who fired the shot that pierced Melton's brain." W.S. Melton, of Paris, Texas, introduced the cartridge case ejected from the murder weapon and the .45-90 bullet that had lodged inside the restaurant building after passing through his brother's head. Ben Vann testified to Goldsby's statement during the dance at Ike Rogers' home, "I didn't intend to kill Melton, only shot to scare him." Deputy Smith testified that, while bringing the outlaw from Nowata on the train and discussing the Lenapah murder with him, "Goldsby said, 'I don't see how they can prove the killing on me, for there were others shooting besides me.'"[6]

The prosecution sealed its case with the testimony of Bert Gray, manager of the Egan Brothers store at Sapulpa. Somewhere, Goldsby had disposed of the .45-90 murder rifle, evidenced by his purchase of the handsome .40-90 Winchester and cartridges from Gray shortly after the Lenapah tragedy. Also, the outlaw had left his old clothes and hat at the store and purchased a new wide-brimmed hat and a coat, which he was wearing when captured. Lawyer Reed's prying brought an admission from Gray that it wasn't the first time he had furnished guns and ammunition to Cook gang members.

As Clarence O. Warren explained, in his 1937 interview, "They would usually come in when my uncle Bert was alone, present their six-shooters, muzzles toward my uncle, and tell him what they wanted and how much. Of course, they got it, and on short order. But they always asked my uncle to keep account of the bill, and the unusual thing about it, they always slipped in when they had money and paid it."[7]

Asked by Judge Parker for an explanation, Gray replied, "Judge, when fellows like that come in and put their guns on you, that makes their credit mighty good with me."[8] That created considerable laughter in the courtroom, the only humorous note throughout the trial.

Still, Reed "worked every inch of ground, contesting step by step, and never wavered an iota."[9] In an attempt to win sympathy for the territory's most cold-blooded killer, he introduced and paraded before the jury Cherokee Bill's "loyal family" which had come to help him in his darkest hour—his mother; his tearful old childhood nurse, Amanda Foster; his brother, Clarence; and the stepsister whose husband he had slain for being mean to him.

Judge Parker instructed the jury the morning of February 27, and the jury rendered the verdict: "Guilty as charged in the within indictment."

Cherokee Bill simply smiled, but his mother broke into wails of grief. "What's the matter with you?" he admonished, harshly. "I'm not dead yet!" In the federal jail that afternoon, he was "engaged in a game of poker with Bill Cook and several kindred spirits, as if nothing had happened."[10]

On March 28, the people of Indian Territory hailed the announcement that the last members of the Cook gang had gone to meet their chums. Verdigris Kid, George Sanders, and a youth named Sam Butler rode into Braggs, nine miles south of Fort Gibson, and "captured the town before breakfast." Before the town marshal Ed Barbee "knew who they were, he had been covered with Winchesters and disarmed." The gang marched him and a few citizens on the street to the front of Thomas J. Madden's

...CLERK'S OFFICE...

U. S. Courts,
Western District of
Arkansas...

STEPHEN WHEELER ... Clerk

Fort Smith, Ark............................189—

We the jury find the defendant Crawford Goldsby alias Cherokee Bill guilty of Murder as charged in the within Indictment. Martin English.

Foreman

Jury verdict in the Ernest Melton murder case.

general store. Sam Butler remained on guard at the door. McWilliams and Sanders entered and took Clerk Joe Morris into custody. Informed that Madden had not yet arrived, but was due any moment, the robbers "decided to wait for him to come and open the safe."

From his home, Madden saw the commotion in front of the store. He "started to make a fight himself," but his wife insisted that he notify Indian Deputy Sheriffs Hiram Stephens and Johnson Manning, who lived a short distance away.

Inside the store, McWilliams and Sanders "leisurely took such goods as they wanted...had a suit apiece and were picking out some gloves," when Butler warned of the approach of the Indian officers. "Butler fired first, killing Manning's horse. The officers fired a volley almost simultaneously, and McWilliams, who sought shelter behind Manning's fallen mount, fell dead, shot in the center of the breast." Sanders and Butler retreated toward their horses, keeping up a steady fire. Clerk Morris ran from the store "to take part...and was fatally wounded in the abdomen" by one of the robbers. Ed Barbee dashed between the deputies and the robbers, secured McWilliams' Winchester, and joined the fight. Halfway to the horses, Sanders fell, "a bullet hole in his temple and several wounds in his body." Butler reached his horse and escaped.[11]

Afterwards Deputy Marshal John Davis tracked Butler to the home of his wife and mother near Island Ford on the Verdigris, southeast of Claremore. The outlaw was lying under an apple tree in the yard as Davis approached. He sprang to his feet and fired a pistol ball into the deputy's right side. Davis fell from his horse but managed to regain his feet and return the shot, striking the outlaw in the breast, killing him instantly. Davis died an hour later.[12]

The remains of Verdigris Kid and Sanders were delivered to Marshal Crump at Fort Smith at noon, and "exhibited in boxes to thousands of people." Stephens and Manning claimed the reward. Deputy Marshal Joe Casaver "identified the revolver that McWilliams was carrying when killed as the one taken from him during the Correta train robbery....McWilliams had cut his name

in the ivory handle." Bill Cook was brought from jail to see his former comrades. "Laying his hand affectionately upon McWilliams'
coffin, he said, 'This is the Kid.'" The bodies were then released
to relatives.[13]

Saturday morning, April 13, Cherokee Bill was brought before
Judge Parker to be sentenced for the murder of Ernest Melton.
The time of sentencing had been made known to few, as the large
crowd which the event would attract was not desirable. The prisoner was accompanied by Lawyer Reed, who alleged five errors on
which he felt the outlaw deserved a new trial. Judge Parker overruled his application, and Reed announced his intention to
appeal. Judge Parker recognized that privilege, then addressed
Cherokee Bill, in part, as follows:

> From the evidence in the case there can be no
> doubt of your guilt. That evidence shows a killing
> of the most brutal and wicked character....Melton
> was the innocent, unoffending victim of the savage
> brutality which prompted the robbery and mur-
> der....From the information that has come to me,
> this murder is one of three committed by you and
> the others were equally as wicked and unpro-
> voked....
>
> Happily for the peace of the country, the whole
> of the band in which you belonged has been bro-
> ken up...killed by officers while in the act of com-
> mitting crimes, or in resisting arrests, and this has
> all happened to them in less than a year.
>
> Now it behooves you to prepare to meet your
> fate. You must reflect on your past life, and fully
> comprehend its wickedness, and the injuries that
> your acts have done others....You must seek for-
> giveness from the author of all mercy, the good
> God, whose government is so much higher than
> human government that he can forgive the worst

of crimes. Then I ask you to consider that no one
can doubt the justice of your conviction, or the
certainty of your guilt, so you can enter upon a
new existence with your sins, wickedness and
crime behind you. Do everything you can to
accomplish this end, and lose not a moment's
time....

It is the duty of this court to pass the sentence
upon you, which under the law follows such a conviction, and which public justice demands....[14]

Asked if he had anything to say why that sentence should not
then be passed, Cherokee Bill replied boldly and defiantly, "No,
sir." Then followed the dread pronouncement, setting June 25 as
the date for his execution.

Cherokee Bill "took the sentence very calmly...disclosed no
emotion whatever. The only show he made that he regarded the
matter more seriously than when he was convicted, was the
absence of his smile."[15]

On April 29, paying the expenses from his private funds, Reed
appealed to the United States Supreme Court, listing fourteen
"manifest errors to the prejudice and great damage" to himself
and his client.[16]

Bill Cook was no longer the most talked-about outlaw of the
day. On April 30, Marshal Crump and five deputies entrained for
the Albany, New York, penitentiary with the erstwhile bandit king
and nineteen prisoners. During a stop at Springfield, Missouri,
Cook "talked gaily to the crowd that struggled to get to his barred
window in the prison car, as if he were on a brief vacation," and
offered pictures of himself for sale. He did not sell any, but gave
one to a *Springfield Democrat* reporter "with the understanding that
he write him up and send a copy to the New York newspapers."
Asked if he thought Crawford Goldsby would be hanged on June
25, he replied, "No bars can hold Cherokee."[17]

Judge Isaac Parker on the bench.

XIV

"Damn a Man Who Won't Fight for His Liberty"

Bill Cook's opinion bore some truth.

On June 25, the Melton case was still in the hands of the Supreme Court. Judge Parker issued a stay of execution, and set July 25 as the new date for the hanging of Cherokee Bill. Lawyer Reed was taking no chances; he appealed to President Cleveland for a commutation, presenting seven sworn affidavits to show that Crawford Goldsby could not have committed the murder for which he had been convicted. President Cleveland agreed to examine the matter.

Cherokee Bill was kept with other condemned prisoners on the lower floor of the federal jail, called "Murderers' Row." Fifty-nine men were then under sentence of death, most of them awaiting results of appeals. J.D. Berry, a former deputy sheriff of Franklin County, Arkansas, was head jailer and as competent as any man who served in that capacity during Judge Parker's tenure. When

Jailer J.D. Berry and his guards, United States Jail, Fort Smith: (1) Duke Brown, Night Guard; (2) Campbell Eoff, Turnkey; (3) Clarence Owensby; (4) Will Lawson; (5) Bras Parker; (6) William Franklin; (7) W.H. McConnell; (8) Robert Jackson; (9) J.D. Berry, Jailer; (10) Tom Parker; (11) Con Berry, Turnkey.

he took charge on November l, 1894, he had 209 prisoners to con-
tend with, and the number had increased considerably by the
spring of 1895.

To make matters worse, the government had reduced the number of guards to ten to cut expenses. Hardly a week passed that
some scheme was not afoot for a single escape or multiple delivery. Nearly all were nipped in the planning stage due to the
inspection system Berry put in effect. Routine inspections had
turned up everything from iron knucks, three-cornered files, and
slingshots to pistols, smuggled in by friends, wives, and sweet-
hearts in cakes, pies, loaves of bread, or hidden under petticoats
and in jugs of buttermilk.

Murderers' Row consisted of two rows of cells running back to
back, north and south down the center of the inner corridor, or
"bullring." The whole inner part of the floor was built of chilled
steel, the doors of cross-barred steel, and the walls of the outer
corridors flanking the bullring on the east and west sides were
crossed as open grates. The prisoners were permitted to mingle
and exercise in the corridors during the day, and were locked in
separate cells at night. With a new execution date set and no word
from the President or Supreme Court, Cherokee Bill grew
morose and unruly. He lorded over the other prisoners, and
among themselves they predicted that something terrible was
about to happen.

Jailer Berry read their mood and sensed trouble brewing. On
July 10, he ordered a search of the entire prison. In Cherokee
Bill's cell, the guards found nine .45 cartridges, and in the bathroom on the Row, hidden in a bucket of lime, a .45 revolver, fully
loaded. A surly Cherokee Bill denied knowing who had smuggled
the gun and cartridges, and the matter, for his part, ended there.
What could you do with a man already convicted for two robberies, under sentence of death for murder, and with a charge of
killing his brother-in-law still on the court docket?

Sherman Vann, a black trusty serving ninety days for larceny,
was arrested and confessed to a conspiracy on the part of sever-

al prisoners to break jail. "At 7:30 of an evening the guards, except one, were usually in the jailer's office on the second floor, and disconnected from the jail by the hallway. At this time the leaders of the plot were to present pistols through the grating of the prisoners' corridor and compel the guard to deliver the keys. Doors were then to be opened and, a friend with more arms was to be at the side room of the jail [entrance to the Row] to assist the prisoners in getting out. Outside the stone wall enclosing the jail were to be several parties heavily armed to assist the escaping prisoners across the Arkansas River, where horses were to be in readiness....Cherokee Bill was at the head of the plot." But Vann said he knew nothing of how the revolver and ammunition had come into the jail.[1]

Another version blamed a trusty named Ben Howell. Howell bore the reputation of being a confederate to the old Dalton gang, but had been serving ninety days for the lowly offense of stealing groceries. He had escaped July 1, had not been recaptured, and was believed to have "smuggled the revolver and ammunition in the bucket of lime on June 27."[2]

It also was suggested that the killer-bank robber Henry Starr was involved. Starr, however, maintained that the newspapers "wronged him" in connecting him, with the plot and had prejudiced his case before the Supreme Court. Starr had been "on good behavior for a long time," and "many of the guards believed him."[3]

What the guards failed to discover—and probably Vann and Starr did not know—was that a second loaded revolver and additional ammunition had been smuggled to Cherokee Bill. He had hidden them behind a loosened stone in the wall of his cell. Most of the inside of the stone had been broken off and the whitewashed end replaced. The ruse thus went unnoticed.

At 6:00 the evening of July 26, the night guards relieved the day guards at the jail, 6:15 being the time for locking up the prisoners on all three floors for the night. This was accomplished on the two upper floors without incident, and guards Bras Parker, William

"Uncle Bill" McConnell, and Will and George Lawson relaxed on the ground outside, a few feet from the entrance to the Row and the stairway to the jailer's office on the second floor. Jailer Berry had been gone about ten minutes.

It was the responsibility of turnkey Campbell Eoff (pronounced "Oaf") and Guard Lawrence "Larry" Keating, who guarded the jail in the daytime, to "ring in" the prisoners on the Row before going off duty. Owing to the long summer days and hot weather, the prisoners were allowed to remain in the corridors until seven o'clock. At that time, the gong was sounded, and after every prisoner had closed the door to his cell, the guard pulled a lever, or "brake," connecting with a long bar which fastened the closed doors of each row of cells at the top. This made it comparatively safe for the turnkey, after laying aside his arms, to enter the bullring and lock each cell individually.

The armed guard walked along the outer corridor to protect him in any emergency, shooting through the grate, if necessary.

There was a flaw in this arrangement. The brake on either row of cells could be thrown back by a broomstick or similar instrument in the hands of a prisoner at the north end of the tiers. On this occasion, in a plot on the part of several prisoners, and unknown to Eoff and Keating attending the cells on the east side, someone threw back the brake on the west tier, releasing the cell doors on the side where Cherokee Bill was confined.

After securing the doors on the east side, Eoff passed around the south end of the tiers to lock those on the west side, Keating keeping pace in the outer corridor, the grate between them. In the third cell from the end, free to push open the door and armed with his smuggled revolver, Cherokee awaited the coming of the officers.

The first cell was empty. The cell adjoining the killer on the south was occupied by Dennis Davis, a half-witted man convicted of murdering Solomon Blackwell in a quarrel over his share of a crop of sorghum. The keyhole of Davis' cell lock had been stuffed with paper, and Eoff's key became fastened in the door. Turning slightly, he remarked to Keating, "Something is wrong here." Keating moved closer, attention momentarily diverted to the trouble.

At that instant, Cherokee Bill sprang from his cell, shoved the muzzle of his revolver through the grate at Keating, and shouted, "Throw 'em up and give me that pistol damn quick!"

Had Keating complied, the killer would have held both officers under subjection. Commanding silence, Bill would have freed his fellow murderers and unlocked the door leading out of the corridor in a wholesale break from the Row. With Eoff's and Keating's lives at stake, forcing the guard remaining outside to surrender their weapons "would have been the work of but a moment.…The next move was to lead the gang up the stairs to the jailer's office, where was a arsenal sufficient to equip the entire lot.…What monstrous and petty crimes that might have been committed in Fort Smith before dawn are too horrible to contemplate.…In spite of its handful of police, that night's work in Fort Smith would doubtless have been the most villainous, terrible and heartrending in the history of any city in America."

Instead, the fearless Keating "acted not only for his friends but for the honor of his country." He reached for a six-shooter, and Cherokee Bill shot him in the stomach. Keating staggered backward and stumbled up the west corridor to give the alarm. Cherokee fired a second shot at him and he fell on the stone floor. The "blood-thirsty criminal then turned his gun on Eoff."

Meanwhile, George Pearce—under death sentence with his brother John for the robbery-murder of a young Texan named William Vandever, and one of the ring-leaders of the plot—leaped from his cell with a leg from a broken table to club Eoff. "This, perhaps, saved the turnkey's life, as Cherokee Bill could not shoot at him without endangering Pearce."

Unarmed and helpless, Eoff ran around the south end of the tiers and up the east corridor. Pearce pursued him with the table leg. When the shots rang out, guards Bras Parker, McConnell, and Will and George Lawson rushed to the Row entrance, and the timely arrival of Parker and George Lawson at the north end of the east corridor enabled Eoff to reach safety. They fired at Pearce, driving him back around the south end of the cells.

McConnell and Will Lawson ran to the fallen Keating. Lawson picked up the revolver he had dropped, asking, "Are you hurt, Larry?" Keating gasped, "Kill the dog, Will, he has killed me," gasped again, and was dead.

Deputy Heck Bruner, with a shotgun, joined Will Lawson and McConnell. They raked the corridor with bullets and buckshot and drove Cherokee Bill back into his cell. With the door partially opened, the killer could cover the corridor and, at an angle, the front of the jail with little danger to himself. The officers' bullets struck the door and ricocheted through the jail without effect. Cherokee Bill returned their shots at random. When his revolver was empty, he reloaded, and started shooting again. Each time he fired, he gobbled his unearthly death cry.

"The excitement rapidly spread to the city. By some common intuition everyone seemed to understand what the trouble was, and police and dozens of armed citizens hastened to help the guards." Jailer Berry reached the scene, and Marshal Crump hurried from his home in the suburbs to take charge. "The gunsmoke was so dense the guards could not see Cherokee Bill and could only fire at the flashes from his weapon." The rest of the prisoners in the unlocked cell "might have come out with Pearce in the corridor, but were too badly frightened," and like those locked in on the east tier, "huddled beneath their bunks or on the floor."

Imbued with the lust of battle, Cherokee Bill "sniped at every form he could see. Jim Shannon and another man were fired upon as they were carrying Keating's remains outside." Keating had served as guard at the jail for nine years and was a very popular citizen of Fort Smith. He had left a wife and four children. "The spirit of vengeance boiled in many breasts....The people wanted to rush the cell and kill Cherokee Bill then and there, but undoubtedly more blood would have been shed....Reason finally triumphed."

Marshal Crump insisted, "Save him for the gibbet."

Jailer Berry "endeavored to induce the killer to surrender. A steady refusal was the only response." The sniping match continued for several minutes. Then a strange thing happened. Henry Starr, who occupied the north end cell on the west side, called to Berry, "If your guards will not fire upon me, I will take Bill's pistol."

Starr was suspected of throwing the brake that had freed the cell doors, but no one had seen him in the act. Doubtful, but impressed by the offer, Berry ordered a cease fire. "Starr walked to the cell, induced Cherokee to give up his weapon, then walked to the end of the corridor and handed it out to the officers." What passed between the two killers was never known, except for Starr's statement to reporters afterwards: "I said, 'Bill, you can't get out...why kill a lot of people?' He replied, 'I'm going to kill every white man in sight. I'll kill you if you come any closer.' If Bill had one soft spot, it was his devotion to his mother. I said, 'Your mother don't want you to kill more than you have already. Why hurt her more?' My plea to give up his pistol for her sake touched him. 'Take it,' he said and handed over the gun."

It seemed so simple.

Even now the guards approached Cherokee Bill cautiously. He was taken from his cell, searched, and the cell given a "thorough overhauling." A small tobacco sack half full of .38 cartridges was found. Cherokee was then "shackled and locked in," and sat on the edge of the iron cot "in bitter disappointment at the failure of his plan."

Outside, the crowd had assumed alarming proportions. The cry "Lynch him! Hang him!" persisted. The killer heard the shouts, and pleaded for the protection of the law he had so many times outraged.

He implored Marshal Crump, "Don't let them have me. I didn't want to kill Keating. If I hadn't shot him, he would have shot me. If I could have captured the jail, no one would have been killed. *Damn a man who won't fight for his liberty.*"

Henry Starr.

Jailer Berry asked if his stepsister, who had been in Fort Smith several days and visited him twice, had furnished him the revolver.

Cherokee Bill replied, "No, it was Ben Howell. He brought me two pistols. The other was found by your guards two weeks ago."

Neither Berry nor Crump believed him.[4]

The deputy marshals and guards worked until midnight restoring order in the jail and dispersing the sightseers. The lynching fever continued unabated. People thronged the streets and public places. District Attorney Read and a number of prominent citizens mingled with the crowds, arguing against mob violence and promising that the case would be vigorously prosecuted. The night passed without incident, but the people remained in a mood of sullen anticipation.

Said one Fort Smith newspaper:

> Lynch law is to be deplored in any community... but this is one case where the people are justified in taking the law into their own hands....Cherokee Bill should have been taken from the jail and hanged to a limb, for that is the fate that such hyenas deserve....His crimes are too numerous and atrocious. He should have been hanged according to the sentence of the law, as an appeal in his case was only to delay justice, yet it has given the monster a chance to murder another man, and deprive a mother and her children of a protector.[5]

XV

"May God Have Mercy on Your Soul"

District Attorney Read moved quickly to make good his promise. Lawyer Reed doubted that Cherokee Bill could be tried for Keating's murder since the judgment and sentence of death in the Melton case was still pending in the Supreme Court and in full force against him. Judge Parker promptly set the matter to rest: the case "stood the same as if he had never been sentenced—there was nothing to prevent his trial on any other charge"; the grand jury "could take up the [Keating] case at once and report their findings."[1]

The court term began at nine o'clock Monday morning, August 5, with 193 criminal prosecutions on the docket, many of which had yet to be presented for indictments. In addition, there had been twenty-five new jail arrivals since July 26, including the recaptured trusty Ben Howell. Howell adamantly denied smuggling in the revolver used to kill Keating and said the relations between himself and Cherokee Bill were never pleasant. He was given an additional six months for breaking jail.

For the first time in three years the grand and petit juries were empaneled on the opening day, and Judge Parker delivered the most lengthy, forceful, and famous grand jury charge during his tenure on the Fort Smith bench. The more important points illustrate his concern for the conditions in Indian Territory, due primarily to such desperados as Cherokee Bill:

> The duties of this grand jury are much more onerous than those of a federal grand jury usually are. Most federal courts only deal with cases directly affecting their government, but here we have nearly all the Indian Territory attached to this jurisdiction, and the laws of the United States are extended over it, to protect that country which for years has been cursed with criminal refugees…who by their acts and their influence have made a hot-bed of crime.…
>
> We are almost submerged in a sea of blood.… The greatest question of the hour is "Can we properly enforce the law?"
>
> I want you to return indictments in every case wherein it is probable that a murder has been committed, and first, I want you to take up the case of one Crawford Goldsby, alias Cherokee Bill, who has been regularly convicted in this court of a foul murder, but upon which the sentence was set aside by his appeal to the Supreme Court.…In the interests of good government, and humanity…something must be done to hold these characters in check.
>
> It is not the severity of punishment, but the certainty of it that checks crime. The old adage of the law, "certainty of punishment brings security," is as true today as it ever was.…

> All criminals are entitled to a fair trial by an
> impartial jury, and that I am sure they will get
> here.[2]

When the grand jury had retired to began deliberations, Judge
Parker turned to the petit jury. He questioned them particularly
as to their scruples against or in favor of capital punishment. One
juror expressed his opposition and was excused. Then, in a brief
charge, the judge said, "We want jurors who will do their duty hon-
estly; who, when the proof shows guilt, will convict, and will acquit
when the proof shows the accused to be innocent. When a man
has done his whole duty he has climbed to the highest summit of
good citizenship."[3]

The grand jury first took up the killing of Larry Keating, as
directed. Within thirty minutes, they indicted Crawford Goldsby
for murder—the quickest indictment ever returned in the court's
history.[4] The court then was adjourned for noon recess.

At one o'clock, Cherokee Bill was arraigned before Judge
Parker. When his shackles were removed, he "'threw back his
head with a quick jerk and took in every detail of the courtroom
at a glance," apparently looking for any avenue of escape. The
faces of the spectators "blanched in anticipation," but the outlaw's glance also took in Court Bailiff Arch Stockton standing
close behind him with a heavy billy, alert and ready to smash him
to the floor. Perhaps, too, the outlaw remembered the iron poker
wielded by Ike Rogers at the time of his capture. "A look of resignation overspread his features and he doggedly awaited
results."[5]

He pleaded not guilty when the indictment was read, and
Parker asked Lawyer Reed, "Are you ready for trial?"

Reed answered, "Your Honor, I know nothing more of the facts
in this case than I have learned through the press. My client has
been locked in his cell and I have had no opportunity to consult
with him. I would like to have until Monday morning to
announce."

Judge Isaac Charles Parker, during the last years of his tenure on the Fort Smith bench (1894-1896).

Judge Parker ruled, "I think this case should be disposed of at once. All the circumstances call for speedy action. I will set it for ten o'clock Thursday morning [August 10], and I want it distinctly understood the case will go on trial then."[6]

Reed gestured as a man "helplessly put upon," picked up his silk hat, and left the courtroom.[7]

On August 8, the consummate Reed laid before Parker a motion for continuance. The document railed against the friends of Keating who had gathered about the jail the night of the killing; "the threats that were made and repeated and continued to be made to lynch this defendant"; "the strangest and most bitter prejudices that exist throughout this city"; "the daily papers of said city and papers for a hundred miles around that have denounced this defendant as a red-handed murderer who should suffer death."

It added, "Since the day of the alleged killing defendant has been night and day confined in irons or shackles in the inner cell of the jail, which has caused defendant great pain and suffering"; "defendant has not been permitted to have or receive any mail matter or communications from friends or any other person, and up to this time has not been able to have more than thirty minutes consultation with his attorney"; "when carried once to this court to be arraigned…hundreds of people assembled in and about said court to gawk and gaze at defendant as if at any moment to seize him and take his life, having a direct tendency and influence against defendant to have a fair and impartial trial.

"Defendant for these reasons prays the court now to continue the trial of this case until the next term…that defendant may have time to prepare his defense, and that said prejudices…may abate and be removed."[8]

Trying to control his personal feelings, Judge Parker assured Reed that his client could get a fair trial and denied his application. The case would go forward as scheduled.

Goldsby was brought into court at ten o'clock Thursday morning, August 10, but the spectators who crowded the room for the proceedings were disappointed—temporarily. Lawyer Reed was not present; he was engaged in a hearing in commissioners court. Judge Parker reset the trial for two o'clock in the afternoon, and the prisoner was taken back to jail.

An even larger crowd was at the afternoon session. Every available space had been taken. Even the jurors had to stand until called to the box. The clanking of chains heralded the coming of Cherokee Bill, and the spectators strained for a glimpse of the desperado. Handcuffed and shackled, under heavy guard, and accompanied by his counsel, he took his place at the long table where prisoners were generally seated. The case was called at once, and the government, through Assistant District Attorney John B. "Buck" McDonough, announced ready for trial.

When Judge Parker asked if the defense was ready, Reed handed him a demurer alleging that the court was without jurisdiction "in view of the fact that the killing occurred in the United States jail." Parker became indignant. "As a legal and common sense proposition," he said, the jail was on government ground; the allegation set forth was "wholly false and without foundation"—an attempt "to drive a wedge that might, by some 'hook or crook,' succeed in putting off the trial to as late a date as possible." The demurrer was overruled, Reed excepted, and the panel of jurors was ordered called.[9]

Judge Parker took unusual precaution in questioning each juror. Though admitting having read of the case and heard it spoken of repeatedly, all declared they were not prejudiced and could render a verdict in accordance with the evidence and the law. "Then," said the Judge, "you are qualified." Of the twelve finally chosen, six lived at least forty miles and six lived farther than 100 miles from Fort Smith. Reed was entitled to twenty preemptory challenges and exhausted every one of them. Still, he was not satisfied, "because said jurors had heard and read of this charge, from which they, and each of them, have made up an opinion as to the guilt or innocence of this defendant." Again he was overruled, and excepted.[10]

John B. "Buck" McDonough, Assistant United States District Attorney, Western District of Arkansas, Fort Smith.

In his opening statement, McDonough contented himself with a concise summary of the killing and the circumstances surrounding it. Reed stated that he would await the testimony and evidence, then judge what offense, if any, had been committed.

Turnkey Eoff described the killing of Keating. He was followed to the stand by Jailer Berry, Will Lawson, Deputy Bruner, and others—the testimony of any one of them being sufficient to convict. Colonel Ben T. DuVal, who had come to the area as a boy in 1829 and was the acknowledged authority on the struggling days of Fort Smith and the early history of the court, testified that the jail was within the court's jurisdiction—Reed attempted to discredit the witnesses by questioning whether some of them "had not offered, just after the alleged killing, to engage with the mob and lynch the defendant." Judge Parker overruled each attempt, and the lawyer excepted.[11]

The government rested shortly after six o'clock, and court adjourned. Groups of people gathered at the bottom of the stairs and on the sidewalk. They dispersed only after the prisoner was taken back to jail. All night long they congregated in hotel lobbies and public places to discuss the day's proceedings and express their feelings, but for the most part, agreed that "Cherokee's jury looked as if they were the kind to convict."[12]

The defense opened at nine o'clock Friday morning by placing Jailer Berry's wife on the stand. Mrs. Berry frequently acted as guide to hundreds of women who desired to go through the jail. She was a very sympathetic woman, greatly interested in the criminals confined there, and was considered knowledgeable of the class on Murderers' Row. A few days before the killing, she had escorted a party through the jail. The women were curious to see Cherokee Bill. Heretofore, the desperado had acted kindly toward her and would come to the door of his cell. On this occasion, however, he held up a blanket and required her and each member of the party to pay a dime to see him. From this, Reed attempted to show that his client was temporarily insane—"he would not have put himself on exhibition to the public for a dime." But when McDonough asked, "Mrs. Berry, do you intend to lead this jury to believe that Cherokee Bill was insane?" the woman exclaimed, "Oh, no! He might have been thinking then of a plan to kill one of the guards and escape and, perhaps, had a guilty feeling. He appeared morose and stubborn."[13]

Quickly Reed pointed to Mrs. Lynch, seated near the jury box, her mournful eyes on her manacled and shackled son, and suggested that the ordeal the two had gone through had "temporarily unbalanced this poor Indian boy's mind," else he would not have "put himself on exhibition to the public for a dime."[14]

It was plain that Reed, from the time the demurrer was filed, "had gone into the trial prepared to fight to the last and seemingly was not overawed by the desperate case he had before him."[15]

Ben Duff, a murderer who occupied a cell near Cherokee Bill's, was sworn and questioned as to "any insanity on Bill's part." Duff's response was not what Reed expected. He told of the conspiracy among the prisoners and identified a letter written by Cherokee Bill several days before Keating's death and given to one of the trusties to deliver to a man outside. In the letter, which had fallen into the hands of the officers, Cherokee Bill wrote, "We are whipping the guards, one a day, and next week one of them is going to die." Cherokee Bill, until then "utterly unmoved," hung his head and never looked up again until the defense rested.[16]

It was 2:30 P.M., and Judge Parker allowed each attorney two and one-half hours to sum up his side of the case to the jury. McDonough spoke until 3:30, stressing the courage and loyalty of Keating and the desperate character of the prisoners he had to deal with. Then Reed took the floor, pleading eloquently for acquittal on grounds that, while Cherokee shot at Keating, he had missed him; his bullets had lodged in the wall beyond, and Keating, in fact, had been killed by stray shots from one of the guards. In a flight of oratory, the lawyer endeavored to hold on as long as there was a straw in sight, until the hands of the court clock pointed to six, and Judge Parker banged his gavel.

Reed continued his oration, and Parker rapped again. "Time's up," he said, sharply.

"Just a few minutes more, Your Honor," replied Reed. "Time's up," Parker repeated, sternly. "Court adjourned." Reed took a last appealing look at the jury, snatched his silk hat from the witness table, and dramatically strode from the room.[17]

McDonough began his closing argument to the jury at ten o'clock Saturday morning. He summed up the evidence produced, spoke of the "blood-thirsty gang to which Cherokee Bill belonged," their "reign of terror" in Indian Territory, and the crime they had committed "under the very eaves of this court."[18]

McDonough was a small man, though perfect in build. With his head thrown back, chest heaved forward, eyes flashing and deep voice reaching the yard outside to many who had been unable to obtain entrance to the courtroom, he "looked the very 'Apollo'" as he pounded blow after blow upon crime and its perpetrators in a masterful eloquence that even shadowed J. Warren Reed's.[19]

He then zeroed in on Cherokee Bill:

> To effect his capture, brave men risked their lives. Even after he had been placed within the prison walls…his ferocity prevented docility, and his only thought was to break away that he might return to the scene of bloodshed from which an outraged law had estranged him.…
>
> Failing to work out his plan for escape, he deliberately, without a moment's hesitation, let out the life blood of a fellow being, one who was beloved by all.…Then, nerved by the very scene of the fresh blood he had spilled, he would add other terrors to the occasion by shooting even those who had come to carry away the dead body of the man he had ruthlessly slain.…
>
> And now he comes here, *with his hands steeped in human gore*, with a long list of misdeeds that should

cause even the imps of hell to shudder…and asks
mercy at your hand; mercy! for a series of crimes
that knows no equal among men of the
Nineteenth century; with his heart reeking with
infamy, he pleads for *mercy*; this most ferocious of
monsters, whose record is more atrocious than all
the criminals who have hitherto stood before this
bar; a creature whose very existence is a disgrace
upon nature, a grievous burden to the atmosphere
from which he draws his breath.…

McDonough moved close to the jury box. His voice took on a
milder tone as he spoke of the untimely death of Larry Keating,
loved by his wife, idolized by his children, and respected by all
who knew him. His voice sank almost to a whisper as he closed:
"We cannot allow this murder to go unavenged. You will do your
duty, I have no fear of that, and may God bless you for it."[20]
A subdued ripple of admiration passed over the crowd, and
Judge Parker sat somewhat entranced by the assistant prosecutor's
performance. The judge's instructions were brief. So were the
jury's deliberations. In just thirteen minutes they came back with
a unanimous verdict. Guilty.
Judge Parker complimented them for their speedy action. "You
have done your duty," he said. Then he did something most
unusual. Turning to Bailiff Stockton, he continued: "Take them
over and give them a good dinner; they deserve it!"
Court convened Monday morning at nine o'clock. Under heavy
guard, handcuffed and shackled, Cherokee Bill was brought
before Judge Parker for sentencing. The desperado again took his
seat at the witness table and quietly sized up the crowd that
packed the room to suffocation.
Lawyer Reed promptly handed the judge two documents. One
was a motion for a stay of sentence, the other a bill of exceptions
listing sixteen reasons why the court should grant a new trial. The
allegations were materially the same as set forth in his motion for

continuance denied August 8. In addition, certain evidence had been excluded at the trial which "might have benefited defendant"; at least one government witness had "showed a disposition to lead a lynching bee proposed the night of the murder"; and certain jurors were "not free from prejudice when they decided the case."[21]

Judge Parker asked if he wished to present an argument, and Reed answered that he did not. "I should think not," said the judge. McDonough had nothing to say concerning the allegations, so Parker overruled both motions without comment.[22]

He then ordered the desperado to stand up. "Crawford Goldsby, you have been convicted of the murder of Lawrence Keating. Under the law it becomes the duty of the court to pass upon you the sentence which the law says shall follow a conviction of the crime of murder. Have you anything to say why that sentence shall not now be passed?"

Cherokee Bill, insolent and defiant, said, "No," and the judge continued:

> I once before sentenced you to death for a horrible and wicked murder committed by you while you were engaged in the crime of robbery. I then appealed to your conscience by reminding you of your duty to your God and your soul....You answered it by committing another most foul and dastardly murder. I shall therefore say nothing to you on that line here and now.
>
> You will listen to the sentence of the law, which is that you...be hanged by the neck until you are dead; and that the marshal of the Western District of Arkansas, by himself or deputy or deputies, cause execution to be done in the premises upon you on Tuesday, September 10th, 1895, between the hours of 9 o'clock in the forenoon and 5 o'clock in the afternoon of the same day. And that

you now be taken to the jail from whence you
came, to be there closely and securely kept until
the day of execution....

May God, whose laws you have broken and
before whose tribunal you must then appear, have
mercy on your soul.[23]

XVI

"A Good Day to Die"

J. Warren Reed again appealed to the United States Supreme Court, listing eighteen errors addressing themselves to the district court's refusal to grant the application for continuance, denying the request to summon certain witnesses at government expense, and its rulings in accepting or rejecting jurors and admitting or rejecting certain testimony.[1] The Vinita *Indian Chieftain* of August 29 noted, "It will insure Cherokee Bill a longer lease on life but the general impression is that it will be a very short one."

By September 10, the Supreme Court had not acted on the appeal and Judge Parker was forced to issue a stay of execution. No publicity, evidently, was given the matter, for that day some 500 to 600 people from a radius of seventy-five miles, mostly from Indian Territory, assembled in Fort Smith to witness the hanging of Cherokee Bill. "They remained at the jail yard the greater part of the morning, despite the assurances of Jailer Berry that the execution would not take place." Attempts to scatter the crowd failed. In the afternoon, "a trusty was shackled, dressed in a long black coat and broad-brimmed hat, and led to the gallows yard in charge of three guards." The crowd "rushed toward the gallows, and finding themselves shut out, many climbed the walls. When

137

they finally realized that Cherokee was not to be hanged, they sorrowfully wended their way homeward."[2]

The *Elevator* and territorial press salved their disappointment: "The case was appealed to the supreme court of the United States upon what is known in law as technicalities—little instruments sometimes used by lawyers to protect the rights of litigants, but oftener used to defeat the ends of justice. It will remain there until the bald-headed and big-bellied respectables who compose that body get ready to look into its merits....Marshal Crump assures us that when the interesting time arrives the execution will be done in public and due notice will be given.[3]

Monday morning, December 2, the Supreme Court delivered its opinion in the Ernest Melton case. "The Judgment of the district court for the Western District of Arkansas in this cause is hereby affirmed."[4] Judge Parker received the announcement by telegram from Washington at 3:00 P.M. Cherokee Bill did not receive the information until a Fort Smith *News-Record* reporter called at the federal jail.

"Cherokee quietly made his appearance at the door of his cell." Told that the Supreme Court had upheld the first conviction for murder against him, "He stood in bewilderment, and seemed somewhat nervous for a few minutes."

"'That ain't very good news, is it Bill?'"

"Not for me, but I guess it is for you Fort Smith people." Asked if he still expected a pardon from the President, he said, "Hell yes," and "began whistling a tune and retired from his cell door to his cot."[5]

Thereafter, he seemed to give little thought to his approaching fate. "He is as reckless and careless as ever...defiant as when the bars first closed behind him...passes all his time playing solitaire...keeps the door of his cell covered with a cloth, which is raised only when no strangers are about. Whenever a visitor enters the jail corridors the cloth goes up, and only the promise now of twenty-five cents will induce Bill to show himself."[6]

Judge Parker did not receive the mandate in the Melton case

until late December. On January 14, Cherokee Bill was brought
before him for resentencing. It was too late for Lawyer Reed to
perform any courtroom histrionics, and in a voice more harsh
than ever, Parker ordered that "the Marshal of the District...take
the said Crawford Goldsby, alias Cherokee Bill, and him safely and
securely keep...until Tuesday the 17th day of March, 1896, and on
that day between the hours of nine o' clock in the forenoon and
five o'clock in the afternoon of said day, cause the said Crawford
Goldsby, alias Cherokee Bill...to be hanged by the neck until he
is dead."[7]

On February 17, 1896, Marshal Crump received a letter from a
kinetoscope company requesting permission to photograph the
execution. The request, forwarded to Washington, was denied,
and on March 12, President Cleveland's new attorney general,
Judson Harmon, instructed Crump "to make the execution private," no cameras allowed. "This disappointed many, as the
Marshal had promised the hanging would be public."[8]

On March 14, Lawyer Reed's last hope was dashed. Attorney
General Harmon sent District Attorney Read a dispatch: "The
President has denied the application for pardon of Crawford
Goldsby, alias Cherokee Bill....The judgment of the court must be
carried out. Acknowledge receipt by telegraph."[9]

Cherokee Bill began preparing for his fate. He accepted reli-
gious advice from the Reverend Father Pius of the German
Catholic Church. Monday morning, March 16, his mother; brother,
Clarence; and old Amanda Foster, who had nursed him in infancy,
arrived at the jail—their first visit since his resentencing. Clarence
was allowed a few words with the prisoner. Cherokee told him, "If
I could hear of Ike Rogers being dead, I would be better satisfied
to die...." Only the mother was permitted to enter his cell. They
talked in low voices a few minutes. Then Lawyer Reed was called
and a will drawn, in which the desperado gave to his mother the
allotment he had claimed in the Cherokee Nation, six miles from
Talala. Clarence Goldsby visited the jail yard and viewed the scaffold and the rope which was being tested by a heavy wooden

dummy. The trap doors of the gallows were thudded open a couple of times to see that they worked properly.[10]

In the afternoon, another document was subscribed and sworn to by Cherokee Bill and attested by Jailer Berry and now Court Clerk Stephen Wheeler.

Following the killing of Keating, a grand jury had spent considerable time questioning prisoners concerning instigators of the jail delivery plot. In August of 1895, Henry Starr, Sherman Vann, Edward and John Shelley, and Edward Shelley's wife, Lu, had been indicted as accessories to the murder. The Shelley brothers had escaped jail in Oklahoma Territory by having a woman on the outside as their confederate; they had been recaptured February 3 near Checotah after an exceedingly hot fight and charged at Fort Smith for assault with intent to kill Deputy Marshal John McCann. Lu Shelley was suspected of passing in the pistol that the guards had found in the bathroom on Murderers' Row on July 10. All five parties had been arraigned and pleaded not guilty. Lu Shelley, with a child only a year and a half old, had been released on bail.[11]

Cherokee Bill made affidavit that neither Henry Starr nor Sherman Vann nor the Shelleys "had anything whatever to do with putting the pistols or pistol...into the jail...used at the time Keating was killed"; that "all plans for said jail delivery were made with other persons whom affiant did not know"; that "affiant first knew that said pistols were to be put into said jail to him by a note that he found in his cell."[12]

The government abandoned its indictment against the Shelleys, Vann, and Henry Starr.[13]

Cherokee Bill retired Monday night at nine o'clock, and reportedly "slept soundly." He was up Tuesday morning at six, whistling and singing, and partook of a light breakfast sent by his mother from her hotel. At 9:30, Mrs. Lynch, Amanda Foster, and Father Pius were admitted to his cell. The hubbub usually heard from the cages was "noticeably lacking"; his fellow prisoners seemed to be impressed with the solemnity of the occasion. To his

Cherokee Bill and his mother, Mrs. Ellen Lynch.

most intimate associates since his confinement, the desperado distributed his few effects.

By 10:30, the corridor was crowded with guards, newspapermen and other privileged individuals, "taking note of every passing incident." Occasionally, Cherokee would throw aside the blanket and appear at the cell door to give some instruction or make some request of the guards. At 11:00 A.M., Marshal Crump, after conversing briefly with the condemned man, announced that the execution would be postponed until 2:00 P.M. to give his stepsister an opportunity to have a few words with him. Maude Brown was due at one o'clock on the Arkansas Valley train.

Outside, an estimated 3,000 sightseers, who had come by rail, wagon, horseback, and afoot, waited to see the outlaw swing. The scene about the yard enclosure and in the streets, "though not disorderly, was one of indescribable excitement." Despite Marshal Crump's order to keep the affair strictly private—with no tickets of admission except to the necessary officials, physicians, clergy, and reporters—hundreds had been provided passes and were gathered at the big gate. A struggling mass of humanity covered the stone walls. The roofs of every available building and shed were occupied. The owners of houses near the jail demanded and received premium prices for space on their roofs and in windows which provided a view of every movement in the prison yard. One rickety shed outside the east wall collapsed under its burden, and there was a "lively scrimmage before those thereon were extricated."

In the jail, Mrs. Lynch, Maude Brown, and Amanda Foster said their good-byes. They strove to restrain their emotions. "Bill was affected...but gave no indication that he was other than perfectly composed."

He told Marshal Crump, "I am ready to go now."

The jail was cleared, and at two o'clock the doomed man was brought forth in handcuffs and shackles. Marshal Crump changed his mind at that moment and told Mrs. Lynch that she could walk with her son. With Cherokee Bill moving slowly because of his leg irons, surrounded by guards Eoff, Will and George Lawson, and Crump in the lead, the march to the gallows began. Mrs. Lynch plodded alongside; Father Pius and the news-papermen brought up the rear.

Cherokee glanced at the crowd atop the walls and buildings, and remarked, "Look at the people; something must be going to happen!"

He noted that it was St. Patrick's Day, and gazing at the sky, added, "This is about as good a day to die as any."

It took only a few minutes for the hundreds holding tickets to gain entrance to the enclosure. By then, the condemned man and guards had mounted the platform of the scaffold. Cherokee glanced at his mother standing near the base of the steps and said, "Mother, you shouldn't have come here." She replied, "I can go where you go."

Marshal Crump read the death warrant. Cherokee gazed over the crowd and showed no emotion. According to legend, when asked if he had anything to say, he replied, "I came here to die, not to make a speech." Actually, he said, "No sir, without he [Father Pius] wants to say a prayer."

Hardened wretch though he was, he "obviously feared going over the dark river without any assistance." The priest offered a brief prayer. Then Cherokee Bill stepped onto the trap.

While Will and George Lawson bound his arms and legs to steady him in case it became necessary, he gazed over the crowd. He recognized many of his acquaintances, and called, "Good-bye, all you chums down that way"—then smiled.

At that moment, a young man in the crowd (though cameras were prohibited) took a snapshot with a Kodak and thrust it quickly back inside his coat. The plate afterwards was finished by photographer John Gannaway, of Fort Smith, and used in making an engraving—the only illustration of the execution.

The black hood was fastened in place, the Lawsons announced "Ready," and Eoff sprung the trap that sent Cherokee Bill "into the undiscovered world." The drop was "scarcely six feet, but the

The Fort Smith *Elevator*, March 20, 1896.

Execution of Crawford Goldsby, alias "Cherokee Bill."

large knot in the noose had been carefully adjusted by the Lawsons, and the neck was broken instantly." Physicians pronounced life extinct, and the mother, who until now had refrained from a demonstration, "wept with little moaning sounds." A few minutes later, the ropes, handcuffs and shackles were removed, the body lowered into a coffin the mother had provided, and borne away, and the crowd dispersed.[14] At the Birnie Brothers Funeral Home, the body was boxed for shipment. At 3:30 in the afternoon, it was put aboard the train. Mrs. Lynch and Maude Brown accompanied it home to Fort Gibson. "Bill was buried next day beside his old chums and companions in crime, Verdigris Kid and Jim French." Mrs. Lynch stated later that, "in compliance with her son's request," the body would be reinterred on the allotment he had willed her near Talala.[15] However, it was never moved from the Fort Gibson cemetery.

Many of the superstitious in Fort Smith and Indian Territory noted the significance of the unlucky number thirteen in the life of Crawford Goldsby. A $1,300 reward was offered for his capture after killing Ernest Melton; his first death sentence was pronounced on April 13; he killed Lawrence Keating on July 26, two times thirteen; he supposedly fired thirteen shots during his fight with the guards; Judge Parker took thirteen minutes to charge the jury in the Keating case; the actual hours used in the trial, August 10–12, numbered thirteen; there were thirteen witnesses for the prosecution; the jury plus the bailiff numbered thirteen; the jury took thirteen minutes to find him guilty; his last thirteen steps were up to the platform of the gallows; he fell through the trap at 2:13 o'clock; and there were thirteen knots in the hangman's noose.

Superstitious others, who believed in the transmigration of the soul, ventured that, sometime, Cherokee Bill would return "in the shape of a horse, a dog or a wild beast, to further annoy the human race."[16] Nonetheless, the Goldsby saga had ended. On March 19, Marshal Crump made his return on the death warrant. On May 18, the Supreme Court disposed of the appeal in the

Keating case: "Crawford Goldsby, alias Cherokee Bill vs. United States, No. 748. In error to the circuit court of the United States for the Western District of Arkansas. The Attorney General, for the United States. No opinion. Dismissed, the cause having abated, on motion by Mr. Solicitor General Conrad, for the defendant in error."[17]

Afterword

George and John Pearce paid the penalty for their crime when they were hanged with another murderer, Webber Isaacs, on April 30, 1896.

On January 4, 1897—a little more than two months after the death of Judge Parker and Congress had reduced his great tribunal to one of comparatively petty jurisdiction over a handful of counties in western Arkansas—the United States Supreme Court reversed the murder case against Henry Starr. At his new trial, on October 6, Starr pleaded guilty to manslaughter and received three years in the penitentiary at Columbus, Ohio. For eight counts of robbery on which he already had been convicted, he was given an additional fifteen years and seven days. He soon convinced prison officials and friends in Indian Territory that he had reformed. He also had been given national publicity for his heroic disarming of Cherokee Bill in the Fort Smith jail. In 1903, President Theodore Roosevelt granted him a full pardon. He returned to the Cherokee Nation and for a time relapsed into respectability. In 1908, he again took the bandit trail, committing numerous bank robberies until finally captured and sent to the Oklahoma state penitentiary in 1915 for a double bank robbery at Stroud. Paroled by Oklahoma's governor in 1919, he starred in a couple of motion pictures but soon reverted to his criminal life, and was killed on February 21, 1921, while robbing a bank at Harrison, Arkansas.[1]

Clarence Goldsby did not forget Cherokee Bill's words in the Fort Smith jail—"If I could hear of Ike Rogers being dead, I would be better satisfied to die." Animosity grew in his breast, and he proclaimed it his lot to mete punishment to his brother's betrayer. Early in 1897, he went to the little town of Hayden, southeast of Nowata, to collect his share of the money being paid Cherokee freedmen from the sale of the Outlet. Ike Rogers was there for the same purpose.

Rogers had received $1,200 of the reward money and still reveled in the glory of having captured Cherokee Bill. Clarence quarreled with him over the wrong done his brother. Rogers held a gun to his head and abused him with vile names and epithets. In turn, Clarence told several friends, "I'm going to kill that damn' Negro marshal." Alex R. Matheson asserted that had Clarence done so at the time he would have been supported by the best citizens of the Cherokee Nation. Retribution was acceptable among the Indians, and nobody liked a Judas. Clarence's friends, however, advised that such an act would only bring him serious trouble and heap more sorrow upon his mother. He was induced to return home and await a future opportunity to draw his money. On April 20, a payment was being made at Fort Gibson, and Clarence was employed as one of the guards. Thousands of people were present, and Ike Rogers was scheduled to arrive on the morning train to help Deputy Bill Smith and other marshals keep order. Clarence waited, and when Rogers alighted on the depot platform, he took deliberate aim with his pistol and sent a bullet into the deputy's neck, killing him instantly. Clarence then dived beneath the coach, crawled out on the other side, and ran into the woods. Deputy Smith led a posse after him. At a point where he thought the fugitive might be intercepted, Smith dismounted. The cunning Clarence waited for him to enter the timber, then mounted the officer's horse and galloped away. No concentrated effort was made to capture Clarence Goldsby, local sentiment being strongly in his favor, and he might have returned to the scene as soon as quiet was restored, without fear of prosecution. Instead, he left the country.

Some believed that he went to Texas, where he was born, and enlisted in the army. Shortly after Oklahoma statehood in 1907, he reappeared briefly at Fort Gibson to see his mother. He then went to St. Louis, where he worked as a Pullman porter until he died of tuberculosis. His body was shipped to Fort Gibson, and he was buried beside his outlaw brother.[2]

Jim Cook became a trusty at the Cherokee National Prison, escaped in December of 1896, and with two others organized a "new Cook gang." On January 28, 1898, Deputy Marshals Gabe Beck and Hess Bussey had a fight with the trio near Inola. Beck was wounded, Cook escaped, and his companions were captured. For the next two years, Cook found sanctuary in the Grand River country around Wagoner. In February of 1900, he obtained a yearling steer from a black man, who had stolen it from a Cherokee freedman, Sarl Harlen. Harlen reclaimed the animal. On March 2, Cook rode to Harlen's house a few miles west of Tahlequah to settle the matter. Harlen opened fire from the door with a Winchester, and Cook, turning to run away, died with three bullets in his back. Harlen was never arrested for the assassination.[3]

Bill Cook became a trusty at the Albany penitentiary. In 1899, he developed consumption. He was allowed to work or not due to his illness, and in January of 1900, asked for a commutation of sentence. On February 7, he died in prison.[4]

Thurman Baldwin received a commutation of his thirty-year sentence from President Roosevelt in July of 1903,[5] and was released from the Detroit House of Corrections in 1904. Elmer Lucas, Curtis Dayson, Jess Snyder, and William Farris served their prison terms. None of the five ever returned to Indian Territory.

Thus ended the Cook gang's saga.

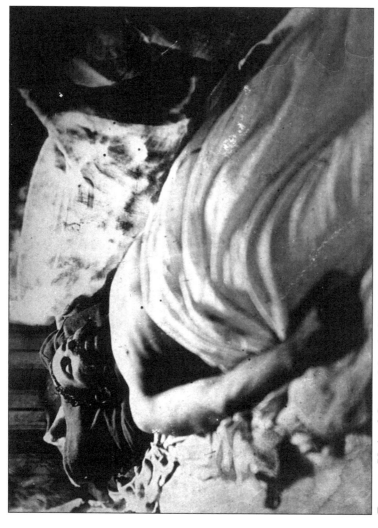

Deputy United States Marshal Ike Rogers in death, slain by Clarence Goldsby, brother of Cherokee Bill.

NOTES

CHAPTER I

1. Letter from Bill Cook, U.S. Jail, Fort Smith, Arkansas, March 16, 1895; S.W. Harman, *Hell on the Border: He Hanged Eighty-Eight Men* (Fort Smith, Arkansas: Phoenix Publishing Company, 1898), 645.

2. Letter from Bill Cook.

3. Ibid.

4. Ibid.

5. Ibid.

6. Harman, 646.

7. Ibid.; Letter from Bill Cook.

8. Letter from Bill Cook.

9. Harman, 646; Eufaula *Indian Journal*, August 10, 1894.

10. Harman, 646–647.

11. Letter from Bill Cook.

CHAPTER II

1. Being light-skinned, Goldsby claimed he came from Alabama and gave his race as "Negro" on his enlistment papers, possibly to qualify as a Buffalo Soldier.

152

2. Harman, 387; "Life Record of Cherokee Bill," *Fort Smith Municipal Police Journal* (annual), 1952, 32; William H. Leckie, *The Buffalo Soldiers: A Narrative* of *the Negro Cavalry of the West* (Norman, Oklahoma: University of Oklahoma Press, 1967), 164; Kaye M. Teall, *Black History in Oklahoma* (Oklahoma City: Oklahoma City Public Schools, 1971), 128.

See also Homer Croy, *He Hanged Them High* (New York: Duell, Sloan and Pearce; Boston: Little, Brown and Company, 1952), 173; J. Gladstone Emery, *Court of the Damned* (New York: Comet Press Books, 1959), 113; Harry Sinclair Drago, *Outlaws on Horseback* (New York: Dodd, Mead and Company, 1964), 174; William Loren Katz, *The Black West* (Garden City, New York: Doubleday and Company, Inc., l971), 199–210.

3. L.B. Bobo, "Reminiscences of Pioneer Days," *Chronicles of Oklahoma*, Vol. 23, No. 3, Autumn 1945, 289; William Taylor interview, *Indian-Pioneer History*, Oklahoma Historical Society, Vol. 10, 349–350; Mrs. E.H. Whitmire, "A Short Sketch of the Life of Cherokee Bill," *Indian-Pioneer History*, Oklahoma Historical Society, Vol. 11, 378.

4. Major J.W. Barlow and Major George L. Gillespie, compilers, *Outline Description of the Military Posts in the Division* of *the Missouri* (Adjutant General's Office, Chicago, April 15, 1876); Herbert M. Hart, *Old Forts of the Southwest* (Seattle: Superior Publishing Company, 1964), 178–79.

5. J. Evetts Haley, *Fort Concho and the Texas Frontier* (San Angelo, Texas: *San Angelo Standard Times*, 1952), 271–274; Grace Bitner, "San Angelo, Texas," *The Handbook of Texas* (Austin: Texas State Historical Association, 1952), Vol. 2, 539–540; Hart, l79.

6. Haley, 270–71.

7. Ibid., 274; Leckie, 163–64.

8. *Galveston Daily News*, March 1, 1878; Haley, 274–75; Leckie, 163–64. Accounts of the affair give Goldsby's name incorrectly as "Goldsbery" and "Goldsbury."

9. Haley, 275; Leckie, 164.

10. Don Rickey, Jr., *Forty Miles a Day on Beans and Hay: The Enlisted Soldier Fighting in the Indian Wars* (Norman, Oklahoma: University of Oklahoma Press, 1963), 143–44.

11. Harman, 387; Mack Stanley, *Hanging Judge and His Desperadoes* (Spiro, Oklahoma: privately printed, 1983), 23.

12. Harman, 387; "Life Record of Cherokee Bill," 32; C.B. Glasscock, *Then Came Oil: The Story of the Last Frontier* (Indianapolis: Bobbs-Merrill Company, 1938), 90; Whitmire, 378; Emery, 113; Stanley, 23.

13. Harman, 406.

14. Jim Etter, "Cherokee Bill's Brother," *True West*, September-October 1974, 14–17, 44.

15. Harman, 387; "Life Record of Cherokee Bill," 35; Stanley, 23.

16. Alex R. Matheson interview, *Indian-Pioneer History*, Oklahoma Historical Society, Vol. 6, 434.

17. Harman, 387; "Life Record of Cherokee Bill," 35; Croy, 174.

18. Letter from Joe Gilbreath, Talala, Oklahoma; quoted in Croy, 174.

19. Frank I. Griffin interview, *Indian-Pioneer History*, Oklahoma Historical Society, Vol. 26, 439–440.

20. J.W. Scott interview, *Indian-Pioneer History*, Oklahoma Historical Society, Vol. 44, 19–21; John M. Reynolds interview, *Indian-Pioneer History*, Oklahoma Historical Society, Vol. 41, 378–79.

21. Lon R. Stansbery, "Cowtown Catoosa, 'Dark and Bloody Ground,' I.T." *Tulsa World*, July 27, 1937; Vinita *Indian Chieftain*, February 14, 1895.

22. Eufaula *Indian Journal*, April 5, 1895.

23. Harman, 391.

24. Stansbery, "Cowtown Catoosa,"

25. James W. Turley interview, *Indian-Pioneer History*, Oklahoma Historical Society, Vol. 11, 51–53.

26. Fort Smith *Elevator*, February 1, 1895; Harman, 394; "Life Record of Cherokee Bill," 34; Croy, 180; Drago, 179.

27. William Byrd interview, *Indian-Pioneer History*, Oklahoma Historical Society, Vol. 1, 482; John C. Humberd interview, *Indian-Pioneer History*, Oklahoma Historical Society, Vol. 5, 287. Humberd served as deputy U.S. marshal at Muskogee, 1891–93.

28. Harman, 389; "Life Record of Cherokee Bill," 33; Glasscock, 91; Stanley, 24.

29. Harman, 389; "Life Record of Cherokee Bill," 33; Glasscock, 91; Croy, 175; William Byrd interview, 482; Humberd interview, 287; Stanley, 24.

30. *United States v. Crawford Goldsby*, No. 1586, U.S. Commissioners Court, Fort Smith, Arkansas, filed March 7, 1894.

31. Tahlequah *Cherokee Advocate*, June 6, 1894; *Oklahoma Daily Press-Gazette*, June 21, 1894.

32. C.W. Slater interview, *Indian-Pioneer History*, Oklahoma Historical Society, Vol. 82, 276–77.

33. Letter from Bill Cook.

CHAPTER III

1. Act of Congress approved March 3, 1893, *U.S. Statutes at Large*, Vol. 27, Chapter 207, 640, Section 10.

2. *Daily Oklahoman,* June 5, 1894.

3. *Oklahoma Daily Press-Gazette,* May 28–29, 1894.

4. Fort Smith *Elevator,* June 1, 1894.

5. Ibid.; *Oklahoma State Capital,* June 12, 1894; *Daily Oklahoman,* June 5 and 12, 1894.

6. *Daily Oklahoman,* June 10, 1894; Eufaula *Indian Journal,* June 15, 1894; Fort Smith *Elevator,* June 15, 1894; Ardmore *State Herald,* June 21, 1894; Burl Taylor interview, *Indian-Pioneer History,* Oklahoma Historical Society, Vol. 10, 320.

7. Muskogee *Phoenix,* June 14, 1894.

8. Harman, 608–609.

9. Ibid., 389; "Life Record of Cherokee Bill," 33; Glasscock, 91; Elizabeth Ross interview, *Indian-Pioneer History,* Oklahoma Historical Society, Vol. 42, 489–90.

10. Fort Smith *Elevator,* June 29, 1894; Harman, 389; Jim Etter, "The Day Sequoyah Houston Fell to Cherokee Bill," *Frontier Times,* October-November 1972; Fielden Salyer Hill interview, *Indian-Pioneer History,* Oklahoma Historical Society, Vol. 29, 129.

11. Etter, "The Day Sequoyah Houston Fell to Cherokee Bill."

12. Ibid.

13. Fort Smith *Elevator,* June 29, 1894; Harman, 389; "Life Record of Cherokee Bill," 33; Glasscock, 92; Stanley, 25.

14. Fielden Salyer Hill interview, 129.

15. Letter from Bill Cook.

16. Fort Smith *Elevator,* June 29, 1894.

17. *Oklahoma State Capital,* June 19 and 21, 1894; *Oklahoma Daily Press-Gazette,* June 21, 1894; Muskogee *Phoenix,* June 21, 1894; *Eufaula Indian Journal,* June 22, 1894; James Calhoun interview, *Indian-Pioneer History,* Oklahoma Historical Society, Vol. 18, 128–29; Amanda L. Still interview, *Indian Pioneer History,* Oklahoma Historical Society, Vol. 10, 164; Etter, "The Day Sequoyah Houston Fell to Cherokee Bill." See also Harman, 389; "Life Record of Cherokee Bill," 33.

18. Harman, 389; "Life Record of Cherokee Bill," 33; Glasscock, 92; Emery, 114; Mrs. E.H. Whitmire, 379. Harman and Emery credit Lou Harden, not Effie Crittenden, with giving Goldsby his nickname.

19. *Oklahoma Daily Press-Gazette,* June 21, 1894.

20. See also *Oklahoma State Capital,* June 21, 1894; *Oklahoma Daily Press-Gazette,* June 21, 1894; *Daily Oklahoman,* June 21, 1894; Eufaula *Indian Journal,* June 22, 1894.

21. Muskogee *Phoenix,* June 21, 1894.

22. Fort Smith *Elevator,* December 7, 1894; Vinita *Indian Chieftain,* December 13, 1894; Harman, 391.

CHAPTER IV

1. Eufaula *Indian Journal*, April 5, 1895.

2. Harman, 660; Tahlequah *Cherokee Advocate*, February 13, 1895; Stillwater *Eagle-Gazette*, February 14, 1895; William Byrd interview, 482.

3. Harman, 660.

4. *United States v. Jas. French*, No.—, U.S. Commissioners Court, Fort Smith, Arkansas, filed February 12, 1890.

5. *United States v. James French*, No. 1151, U.S. Commissioners Court, Fort Smith, Arkansas, filed October 15, 1892.

6. *United States v. James French*, No.—, U.S. Commissioners Court, Fort Smith, Arkansas, warrant issued November 29, 1893.

7. Nowata, I.T., dispatch, July 5, *Oklahoma State Capital*, July 6, 1894; George Bristow, "Hectic Days in Territory, In the Early Nineties," *The Ranchman*, Vol. 2, No. 6, October 1942 (Bristow became station agent at Nowata after Richards was killed); Robert Cotton, "'Cherokee Bill' Was Among Most Bloodthirsty Outlaws," *Nowata Daily Star*, October 12, 1960.

8. Letter from George Bristow to Bill Hoge, "Oolagah Oozings," *Tulsa World Magazine*, December 27, 1959.

9. *Oklahoma State Capital*, July 6, 1894; Stillwater *Eagle-Gazette*, November 29, 1894.

10. Muskogee, I.T., dispatch, July 6, Eufaula *Indian Journal*, July 13, 1894; Stillwater *Eagle-Gazette*, July 19, 1894.

11. Eufaula *Indian Journal*, July 13, 1894.

12. Accounts of the Red Fork holdup appear in *Beaver County Democrat*, July 12, 1894; *Wichita Daily Eagle*, July 20, 1894; *Guthrie Daily Leader*, July 21, 1894 (erroneously gives the location as "Red Rock," in present Noble County, Oklahoma); Eufaula *Indian Journal*, August 10, 1894; Vinita *Indian Chieftain*, November 15, 1894; Lon R. Stansbery, *The Passing of 3-D Ranch* (Tulsa, Oklahoma: privately printed, 1930), 17.

13. Accounts of the Chandler robbery and capture of Elmer Lucas appear in *Daily Oklahoman*, August 1, 1894; *Oklahoma State Capital*, August 1 and 3, 1894.

14. Clarence O. Warren interview, *Indian-Pioneer History*, Oklahoma Historical Society, Vol. 11, 228–29.

15. Sapulpa, I.T., dispatch, August 2, *Oklahoma State Capital*, August 4, 1894; Vinita *Indian Chieftain*, August 9, 1894; Eufaula *Indian Journal*, August 10, 1894; Stansbery, *The Passing of 3-D Ranch*, 17–18. The roles of Allen and Pickett are recapped in *Oklahoma State Capital*, May 19 and June 25, 1903.

CHAPTER V

1. *Tahlequah Telephone*, I.T., dispatch, Ardmore *State Herald*, September 13, 1894.

2. Eufaula *Indian Journal*, September 21, 1894.

3. Muskogee, I.T., dispatch, October 5, Ardmore *State Herald*, October 11, 1894; Tahlequah *Cherokee Advocate*, October 10, 1894; *South McAlester Capital*, October 11, 1894; Stillwater *Eagle-Gazette*, October 11, 1894.

4. Wagoner, I.T., dispatch, October 10, Ardmore *State Herald*, October 18, 1894; Claremore, I.T., dispatch, October 10, Eufaula *Indian Journal*, October 19, 1894.

5. Ibid.; *United States v. Crawford Goldsby, alias Cherokee Bill, and two others*, No. 5057 (Grand Jury indictment—Robbery), U.S. District Court, Fort Smith, Arkansas, filed February 15, 1895.

6. *Kansas City Times*, October 12, 1894.

7. Harman, 646.

8. *Oklahoma State Capital*, September 20, 1894; *Oklahoma Daily Times-Journal*, September 20, 1894; Vinita *Indian Chieftain*, October 11, 1894; Muskogee *Phoenix*, October 17, 1894.

9. *Muldrow Register*, I.T., dispatch, Vinita *Indian Chieftain*, October 11, 1894.

10. Harman, 646.

CHAPTER VI

1. Wagoner, I.T., dispatch, October 22, *Daily Oklahoman*, October 22, 1894; Edmond *Sun-Democrat*, October 25, 1894; Vinita *Indian Chieftain*, October 25, 1894.

2. Ibid.

3. Vinita *Indian Chieftain*, October 25, 1894; Stillwater *Eagle-Gazette*, November 1, 1894; Ardmore *State Herald*, November 1, 1894; Eufaula *Indian Journal*, November 1, 1894.

4. Stillwater *Eagle-Gazette*, November 29, 1894.

5. Wagoner, I.T., dispatch, October 24, *Daily Oklahoman*, October 25, 1894; *Claremore Progress*, October 27, 1894; Ardmore *State Herald*, November 1, 1894; *United States v. Crawford Goldsby, alias Cherokee Bill, and three others*, No. 5050 (Grand Jury indictment—Robbery), U.S. District Court, Fort Smith Arkansas, filed February 14, 1895.

6. Vinita *Indian Chieftain*, October 25, 1894; Stillwater *Eagle-Gazette*, November 1, 1894.

7. Tahlequah, I.T., dispatch, Ardmore *State Herald*, November 8, 1894.

8. *Oklahoma State Capital*, November 15, 1894.

9. Tahlequah, I.T., dispatch, October 27, *Daily Oklahoman*, October 28, 1894.

10. Fort Smith, Arkansas, dispatch, October 26, *Daily Oklahoman*, October 27, 1894; *South McAlester Capital*, November 1, 1894.

11. Wagoner, I.T., dispatch, October 27, Ardmore *State Herald*, November 1, 1894; Eufaula *Indian Journal*, November 2, 1894.

12. Ibid.

13. Fort Smith, Arkansas, dispatch, October 31, *Daily Oklahoman*, November 1, 1894.

14. Grand Jury Report to the Hon. Isaac C. Parker, District Court of the Western District of Arkansas, August term, 1894, dated October 24, 1894; *South McAlester Capital*, November 1, 1894; Ardmore *State Herald*, November 8, 1894.

15. Vinita *Indian Chieftain*, November 1 and 15, 1894; Harman, 648.

16. Wagoner, I.T., dispatch, November 10, *Daily Oklahoman*, November 11, 1894.

CHAPTER VII

1. Washington., D.C., dispatch, October 24, *Oklahoma State Capital*, October 24, 1894; Wagoner, I.T., dispatch, October 24, *Daily Oklahoman*, October 25, 1894.

2. Washington, D.C., dispatch, October 26, 1894; *Oklahoma State Capital*, October 26, 1894; Ardmore *State Herald*, November 1, 1894.

3. Washington, D. C., dispatch, October 25, *Oklahoma State Capital*, October 25, 1894.

4. Ibid.; Washington, D.C., dispatch, October 26, *Daily Oklahoman*, October 27, 1894.

5. Washington, D.C., dispatch, October 26, Eufaula *Indian Journal*, November 2, 1894; Ardmore *State Herald*, November 8, 1894.

6. Washington, D.C. dispatch, October 26, *Oklahoma State Capital*, October 26, 1894; Ardmore *State Herald*, November 1, 1894.

7. Ibid.

8. Quoted in Ardmore *State Herald*, November 8, 1894.

9. Ibid.

10. Ibid.

11. *Oklahoma State Capital*, October 26, 1894; Ardmore *State Herald*, November 1, 1894; Stillwater *Eagle-Gazette*, November 1, 1894.

12. Ibid.; Muskogee *Phoenix*, November 21, 1894.

CHAPTER VIII

1. Jesse McDermott interview, *Indian-Pioneer History*, Oklahoma Historical Society, Vol. 7, 14–15.

2. "How McDermott Was Robbed" (Letter from W.T. Berry to J.D. Berry, November 4, 1894), Fort Smith *Times-Democrat*, November 6, 1894; Ardmore *State Herald*, November 22, 1894.

3. *Oklahoma State Capital*, November 5, 1894; *Daily Oklahoman*, November 6, 1894.

4. *Daily Oklahoman*, November 16, 1894; Stillwater *Eagle-Gazette*, November 22, 1894.

5. Accounts of the Lenapah robbery-murder appear in *Daily Oklahoman*, November 11, 1894; Wagoner, I.T., dispatch, November 10, Ardmore *State Herald*, November 14, 1894.
See also Vinita *Indian Chieftain*, February 28, 1895; *United States v. Crawford Goldsby, alias Cherokee Bill*, No. 106, U.S. District Court, Fort Smith, Arkansas, filed February 8, 1895; *United States v. Crawford Goldsby, alias Cherokee Bill*, No. 5869 (Grand Jury indictment—Larceny of Money of U.S.), U.S. District Court, Fort Smith, Arkansas, filed November 22, 1895; *Goldsby v. United States*, No. 620, December 2, 1895, 16 Supreme Court Reporter 216–19; Harman, 392; "Life Record of Cherokee Bill," 33.

6. Coffeyville, Kansas, dispatch, November 9, *Daily Oklahoman*, November 11, 1894; Wagoner, I.T., dispatch, November 10, Ardmore *State Herald*, November 14, 1894.

7. *United States v. Crawford Goldsby, alias Cherokee Bill*, No. 106, U.S. District Court, Fort Smith, Arkansas, filed February 8, 1895; *Goldsby v. United States*, No. 620, December 2, l895, 16 Supreme Court Reporter 218; Harman, 393.

8. Burl Taylor interview, *Indian-Pioneer History*, Oklahoma Historical Society, Vol. 10, 315–16; Vinita *Indian Chieftain*, November 22, 1894; Fort Smith *Elevator*, November 23, 1894; Stillwater *Eagle-Gazette*, November 29, 1894.

9. Vinita *Indian Chieftain*, November 22, 1894.

10. Fort Smith *News-Record*, November 21, 1894.

11. Claremore, I.T., dispatch, November 19, Eufaula *Indian Journal*, November 23, 1894; Stillwater *Eagle-Gazette*, November 29, 1894.

CHAPTER IX

1. D.M. Wisdom, U.S. Indian Agent, to Henry S. Davis, Washington, D.C., quoted in Ardmore *State Herald*, November 22, 1894.

2. Dispatches from Kansas, Missouri, and Arkansas newspapers in Ardmore *State Herald*, November 22, 1894; *Daily Oklahoman*, November 23, 1894; *Oklahoma Daily Times-Journal*, November 24, 27, and 28, 1894; Stillwater *Eagle-Gazette*, November 29, 1894.

3. Ardmore *State Herald*, November 22, 1894.

4. Muskogee, I.T., dispatches, November 18–19, Ardmore *State Herald*,

November 22, 1894; Harman, 393.

5. Muskogee, I.T., dispatch, November 24, *Daily Oklahoman*, November 24, 1894.

6. Topeka, Kansas, dispatch, November 18, Ardmore *State Herald*, November 22, 1894; *Afton News*, November 23, 1894.

7. The Bellevue fight is amply described in Sergeant W.J.L. Sullivan, Texas Ranger, Company B, Frontier Battalion, *Twelve Years in the Saddle for Law and Order on the Frontiers of Texas* (Austin: von Boeckman-Jones Co., Printers, 1909), 107–12.

8. Wichita Falls, Texas, dispatch, November 22, Wichita (Kansas) *Daily Eagle*, November 22, 1894; Fort Smith *Elevator*, November 23, 1894; Vinita *Indian Chieftain*, November 29, 1894.

9. Sullivan, 112.

10. Vinita *Indian Chieftain*, November 29 and December 13, 1894; Stillwater *Eagle-Gazette*, November 29 and December 6, 1894; Fort Smith *Elevator*, December 7, 1894; Harman, 647.

11. Harman, 650.

CHAPTER X

1. Fort Gibson, I.T., dispatch, November 27, *Daily Oklahoman*, November 28, 1894.

2. Fort Gibson, I.T., dispatch, November 29, Stillwater *Eagle-Gazette*, December 6, 1894.

3. McAlester, I.T., dispatch, November 30, *Daily Oklahoman*, November 30, 1894; *Oklahoma Daily Times-Journal*, November 30, 1894; Ardmore *State Herald*, December 6, 1894.

4. Checotah, I.T., dispatch, December 18, Ardmore *State Herald*, December 27, 1894.

5. *Oklahoma State Capital*, December 26, 1894.

6. Coalgate, I.T., dispatch, December 27, Ardmore *State Herald*, December 27, 1894.

7. Maude Brown Surrell interview, *Indian-Pioneer History*, Oklahoma Historical Society, Vol. 87, 483–84.

8. Also, Claremore, I.T., dispatch, January 5, Ardmore *State Herald*, January 10, 1895.

9. William Taylor interview, *Indian-Pioneer History*, Oklahoma Historical Society, Vol. 10, 350.

10. Claremore, I.T., dispatch, January 1, Eufaula *Indian Journal*, January 4, 1895; Tahlequah *Cherokee Advocate*, January 9, 1895; Claremore, I.T., dispatch,

January 5, Ardmore *State Herald,* January 10, 1895; George Bristow, "Hectic Days in Territory, In the Early Nineties."

    11. Eufaula *Indian Journal,* January 4, 1895; Ardmore *State Herald,* January 10, 1895; Tahlequah *Cherokee Advocate,* January 10, 1895.

CHAPTER XI

    1. Muskogee *Phoenix,* December 22, 1894; *Oklahoma State Capital,* December 26, 1894.

    2. Tahlequah, I.T., dispatch, December 26, *Oklahoma State Capital,* December 26, 1894.

    3. *Oklahoma Daily Star,* December 28, 1894.

    4. Ibid.; *Oklahoma State Capital,* December 29, 1894.

    5. Sullivan details the three-week pursuit in *Twelve Years in the Saddle,* 113–17.

    6. Sullivan, 118.

    7. Ibid., 118–19.

    8. Ibid., 119–20.

    9. Roswell, New Mexico, dispatch, January 13, Eufaula *Indian Journal,* January 18, 1895; *Dallas News,* January 25, 1895; *Daily Oklahoman,* January 26, 1895; Harman, 650–52.

    10. Ibid.

    11. Ibid.

    12. Ibid.

    13. Ibid.

    14. *Oklahoma State Capital,* January 14, 1895; *Oklahoma Daily Times-Journal,* January 15, 1895; *Daily Oklahoman,* January 15–16, 1895; Eufaula *Indian Journal,* January 18, 1895.

    15. Sullivan, 122–23.

    16. Quoted in *Oklahoma State Capital,* January 15, 1895; *Daily Oklahoman,* January 15, 1895.

    17. Sullivan, 123–24.

    18. Eufaula *Indian Journal,* January 25, 1895; Harman, 652.

    19. Fort Smith, Arkansas, dispatch, January 20, *Oklahoma State Capital,* January 22, 1895; Vinita *Indian Chieftain,* January 24 1895; Eufaula *Indian Journal,* January 25, 1895.

    20. Account of the robbery appears in Eufaula *Indian Journal,* January 18, 1895.

    21. Vinita *Indian Chieftain,* January 24, 1895.

22. *Kansas City Times* and Eufaula *Indian Chieftain* quoted in *Oklahoma State Capital,* January 19 and 22, 1895.

23. Fort Smith *Elevator,* March 29, 1895.

24. Dee Harkey, *Mean as Hell* (Albuquerque: University of New Mexico Press, 1948), 94–95. Dee Harkey was a brother of Sheriff J.H. Harkey of Dickens County, Texas, and a deputy United States marshal in New Mexico.

25. James D. Shinkle, *Reminiscences of Roswell Pioneers* (Roswell, New Mexico: Hall-Poorbaugh Press, Inc., 1966), 228-29.

CHAPTER XII

1. Harman, 394, 396; "Life Record of Cherokee Bill," 34–35.

2. Fort Smith *Elevator,* February 1, 1895; Harman, 394–98; "Life Record of Cherokee Bill," 34–35.

3. Fort Smith *Elevator,* February 1, 1895; *Perkins Journal,* February 7, 1895.

4. Harman, 398–99.

5. Fort Smith *Elevator,* February 1, 1895.

6. *Oklahoma State Capital,* February 14, 1895.

7. Harman, 401–402.

8. Ibid.

9. Vinita *Indian Chieftain,* July 25, 1895.

10. Accounts of the Catoosa killings appear in *Oklahoma State Capital,* February 9, 1895; *Daily Oklahoman,* February 9, 1895; Tahlequah *Cherokee Advocate,* February 13, 1895; Vinita *Indian Chieftain,* February 14, 1895; Stillwater *Eagle-Gazette,* February 14, 1895; Harman, 655–57; Stansbery, *The Passing of 3-D Ranch,* 45–46.

11. Vinita *Indian Chieftain,* February 14, 1895.

12. Ibid.

13. Ibid.

14. *United States v. Crawford Goldsby, alias Cherokee Bill,* No. 106 (Grand Jury indictment—Murder), U.S. District Court, Fort Smith, Arkansas, filed February 14, 1895.

15. *United States v. Crawford Goldsby, alias Cherokee Bill, and three others,* No. 5050 (Grand Jury indictment—Robbery), U.S. District Court, Fort Smith, Arkansas, filed February 14, 1895; trial case No. 307.

16. *United States v. Crawford Goldsby, alias Cherokee Bill, and two others,* No. 5057 (Grand Jury indictment—Robbery), U.S. District Court, Fort Smith, Arkansas, filed February 15, 1895; trial case No. 307.

CHAPTER XIII

1. Harman, 158–59.

2. Ibid., 399–400.

3. Transcript of trial, *United States v. Crawford Goldsby, alias Cherokee Bill*, No. 106.

4. Vinita *Indian Chieftain*, February 28, 1895; Harman, 399.

5. Transcript of trial; Harman, 399.

6. Ibid.; Vinita *Indian Chieftain*, February 28, 1895; Eufaula *Indian Journal*, March 1, 1895.

7. Clarence O. Warren interview, 232–33.

8. Ibid.; Transcript of trial.

9. Harman, 400.

10. Ibid.

11. *Oklahoma State Capital*, March 29, 1895; Vinita *Indian Chieftain*, April 4, 1895; *South McAlester Capital*, April 4, 1895; Eufaula *Indian Journal*, April 5, 1895.

12. Vinita *Indian Chieftain*, August 1, 1895.

13. Fort Smith *Elevator*, March 28, 1895; Vinita *Indian Chieftain*, April 4, 1895; Eufaula *Indian Journal*, April 5, 1895.

14. Fort Smith *Elevator*, April 19, 1895; Vinita *Indian Chieftain*, April 25, 1895.

15. Ibid.

16. *United States v. Crawford Goldsby, alias Cherokee Bill*, No. 106 (Petition for Writ of Error), filed May 4, 1895.

17. Vinita *Indian Chieftain*, May 2, 1895; Fort Smith *Elevator*, May 3, 1895; *Springfield* (Missouri) *Democrat* quoted in Ardmore *State Herald*, May 9, 1895.

CHAPTER XIV

1. *Oklahoma State Capital*, July 13, 1895; Vinita *Indian Chieftain*, July 18, 1895.

2. Harman, 402–403; "Life Record of Cherokee Bill," 35–36.

3. *Oklahoma State Capital*, July 13, 1895; Vinita *Indian Chieftain*, July 18, 1895.

4. The foregoing account of the killing of Lawrence Keating and surrender of Cherokee Bill appears in *Oklahoma Daily Times-Journal*, July 27, 1895; Vinita *Indian Chieftain*, August 1, 1895; Fort Smith *Elevator*, August 2, 1895; Harman, 404–10; "Life Record of Cherokee Bill," 36–37.

5. Name and date of newspaper not given, quoted in Harman, 410–11.

CHAPTER XV

1. *United States v. Crawford Goldsby, alias Cherokee Bill*, No. 132 (Motion in

Arrest of Judgment), U.S. District Court, Fort Smith, Arkansas, filed August 3, 1895; Harman, 413.

2. For full text of "The Famous Grand Jury Charge" see Glenn Shirley, *Law West of Fort Smith: A History of Frontier Justice in the Indian Territory, 1834–1896* (New York: Henry Holt and Company, 1957), Appendix E, 245–71. Excerpts in Vinita *Indian Chieftain*, August 15, 1895.

3. Harman, 415; "Life Record of Cherokee Bill," 37.

4. *United States v. Crawford Goldsby, alias Cherokee Bill*, No. 132 (Grand Jury indictment), U.S. District Court, Fort Smith, Arkansas, filed August 5, 1895; Vinita *Indian Chieftain*, August 8, 1895.

5. Harman, 416.

6. Ibid.; Vinita *Indian Chieftain*, August 8, 1895.

7. Croy, 198.

8. *United States v. Crawford Goldsby, alias Cherokee Bill*, No. 132 (Motion of continuance), U.S. District Court, Fort Smith, Arkansas, filed August 8, 1895.

9. Ibid., Demurrer, filed in open court, August 10, 1895.

10. Ibid., Bill of Exceptions, filed August 12, 1895.

11. Ibid., Testimony and Proceedings, August 10–12, 1895.

12. Harman, 421.

13. Testimony and Proceedings, *United States v. Crawford Goldsby, alias Cherokee Bill*, No. 132 (August 10–12, 1895); Harman, 422–23.

14. Ibid.

15. Harman, 420.

16. Testimony and Proceedings, *United States v. Crawford Goldsby, alias Cherokee Bill*, No. 132 (August 10–12, 1895); Vinita *Indian Chieftain*, August 15, 1895; Harman, 423.

17. Harman, 424–25.

18. Ibid., 425–26.

19. Ibid., 429.

20. Full text of McDonough's closing remarks appears in Harman, 425–430.

21. Motion for New Trial and Bill of Exceptions, *United States v. Crawford Goldsby, alias Cherokee Bill*, No. 132, filed August 12, 1895.

22. Harman, 432.

23. Full text of the sentence, considered by some members of the Fort Smith bar to be Judge Parker's masterpiece, appears in Harman, 444–46.

CHAPTER XVI

1. Assignment of Errors, *United States v. Crawford Goldsby, alias Cherokee Bill*,

No. 132, filed August 24, 1895; *Crawford Goldsby, alias Cherokee Bill, Plaintiff in Error, v. United States*, No. 728, 163 U.S. 688, 16 Supreme Court Reporter 1201.

   2. Fort Smith *Elevator*, September 13, 1895.

   3. Ibid.; *Oklahoma State Capital*, September 21, 1895; *Oklahoma Daily Times-Journal*, October l, 1895.

   4. Mandate, Supreme Court of the United States, *Crawford Goldsby, alias Cherokee Bill, Plaintiff in Error, v. United States*, No. 620, December 2, 1895; 16 Supreme Court Reporter 216.

   5. Fort Smith *News-Record*, December 3, 1895; *Oklahoma Daily Times-Journal*, December 4, 1895.

   6. Fort Smith *Elevator*, December 20, 1895.

   7. Sentence for Murder, *United States v. Crawford Goldsby, alias Cherokee Bill*, No. 176, filed January 14, 1896.

   8. Vinita *Indian Chieftain*, February 20 and March 12, 1896.

   9. Attorney General Harmon to United States Attorney Read, March 14, 1896.

   10. Fort Smith *Elevator*, March 20, 1896; Harman, 436.

   11. Fort Smith, Arkansas, dispatch, August 29, *South McAlester Capital*, September 5, 1895; Vinita *Indian Chieftain*, September 5, 1895; Ardmore *State Herald*, September 12, 1895; Fort Smith *Elevator*, September 13, 1895.

   12. Cherokee Bill's Affidavit, March 16, 1896; Harman, 436–38.

   13. Vinita *Indian Chieftain*, April 23, 1896.

   14. Accounts of the execution appear in Vinita *Indian Chieftain*, March 19, 1896; Fort Smith *Elevator*, March 20, 1896; Harman, 439–43; "Life Record of Cherokee Bill," 37–39.

   15. Vinita *Indian Chieftain*, March 26, 1896.

   16. Harman, 444.

   17. U.S. 688, 16 Supreme Court Reporter 1201; Vinita *Indian Chieftain*, March 26, 1896.

AFTERWORD

   1. Glenn Shirley, *Henry Starr, Last of the Real Badmen* (New York: David McKay Company, Inc., 1965).

   2. Muskogee *Phoenix*, April 22, 1897; Alex R. Matheson interview, 435–36; William Taylor interview, 351–52; Harman, 447–49; Etter, "Cherokee Bill's Brother."

   3. Vinita *Indian Chieftain*, April 8, 1897; *Oklahoma State Capital*, January 28, 1898, and March 3, 1900.

   4. Albany, New York, dispatch, January 9, *Daily Oklahoman*, January 10,

1900; Albany, New York, dispatch, February 7, *Oklahoma State Capital*, February 7, 1900; *Daily Oklahoman*, February 9, 1900.

    5. *Oklahoma State Capital*, August 1, 1903.

Bibliography

DOCUMENTS

Act of Congress approved March 3, 1893, *U.S. Statutes at Large*, Vol. 27, Chapter 207, Section 10, 640.

Barlow, Major J.W. and Major George L. Gillespie, compilers. *Outline Description of the Military Posts in the Division of the Missouri* (Adjutant General's Office, Chicago, April 15, 1876).

Cherokee Bill's Affidavit, March 16, 1896.

Crawford Goldsby, alias Cherokee Bill, Plaintiff in Error, vs. United States, No. 728, May 18, 1896; 16 U.S. 688; 16 Supreme Court Reporter 1201.

Grand Jury Report to the Hon. Isaac C. Parker, District Court of the Western District of Arkansas, August term, 1894, October 24, 1894.

Letter from Bill Cook (Autobiographical sketch written in the U.S. Jail at Fort Smith, Arkansas, March 16, 1895).

Supreme Court of the United States, *Crawford Goldsby, alias Cherokee Bill, Plaintiff in Error, vs. United States*, No. 620, MANDATE, December 2, 1895. See also 16 Supreme Court Reporter 216–19.

United States vs. Crawford Goldsby, No. 1586, U.S. Commissioners Court, Fort Smith, Arkansas, filed March 7, 1894.

United States vs. Crawford Goldsby, alias Cherokee Bill, No. 106, U.S. District Court, Fort Smith, Arkansas, filed February 8, 1895.

United States vs. Crawford Goldsby, alias Cherokee Bill, and three others, No. 5050 (Grand Jury indictment—Robbery), U.S. District Court, Fort Smith, Arkansas, filed February 14, 1895; trial case No. 307

United States vs. Crawford Goldsby, alias Cherokee Bill, and two others, No. 5057 (Grand Jury indictment—Robbery), U.S. District Court, Fort Smith, Arkansas, filed February 15, 1895; trial case No. 307.

United States vs. *Crawford Goldsby, alias Cherokee Bill*, No. 106 (Grand Jury indictment—Murder), U.S. District Court, Fort Smith, Arkansas, filed February 14, 1895.

United States vs. Crawford Goldsby, alias Cherokee Bill, No. 106 (Petition for Writ of Error), U.S. District Court, Fort Smith, Arkansas, filed May 4, 1895.

United States vs. Crawford Goldsby, alias Cherokee Bill, No. 132 (Motion in Arrest of Judgment), U.S. District Court, Fort Smith, Arkansas, filed August 3, 1895.

United States vs. Crawford Goldsby, alias Cherokee Bill, No. 132 (Grand Jury indictment), U.S. District Court, Fort Smith, Arkansas, filed August 5, 1895.

United States vs. Crawford Goldsby, alias Cherokee Bill, No. 132 (Motion of continuance), U.S. District Court, Fort Smith, Arkansas, filed August 8, 1895.

United States vs. Crawford Goldsby, alias Cherokee Bill, No. 132 (Demurrer), U.S. District Court, Fort Smith, Arkansas, filed August 10, 1895.

United States vs. Crawford Goldsby, alias Cherokee Bill, No. 132 (Testimony and Proceedings), U.S. District Court, Fort Smith, Arkansas, August 10–12, 1895.

United States vs. Crawford Goldsby, alias Cherokee Bill, No.132 (Bill of Exceptions), U.S. District Court, Fort Smith, Arkansas, filed August 12, 1895.

United States vs. Crawford Goldsby, alias Cherokee Bill, No. 132 (Motion for New Trial and Bill of Exceptions), U.S. District Court, Fort Smith, Arkansas, filed August 12, 1895.

United States vs. Crawford Goldsby, alias Cherokee Bill, No. 132 (Assignment of Errors), U.S. District Court, Fort Smith, Arkansas, filed August 24, 1895.

United States vs. Crawford Goldsby, alias Cherokee Bill, No. 5869 (Grand Jury indictment—Larceny of Money of U.S.), U.S. District Court, Fort Smith, Arkansas, filed November 22, 1895.

United States vs. Crawford Goldsby, alias Cherokee Bill, No. 176 (Sentence for Murder), U.S. District Court, Fort Smith, Arkansas, filed January 14, 1896.

United States vs. Jas. French, No. —, U.S. Commissioners Court, Fort Smith, Arkansas, filed February 12, 1890.

United States vs. James French, No. 1151, U.S. Commissioners Court, Fort Smith, Arkansas, filed October 14, 1892.

United States vs. James French, No. —, U.S. Commissioners Court, Fort Smith, Arkansas, warrant issued November 29, 1893.

NEWSPAPERS

Afton News, November 23, 1894.

Ardmore *State Herald,* June 21, 1894; September 13, 1894; October 11 and 18,

1894; November 1, 8 and 22, 1894; December 6 and 27, 1894; January 10, 1895; May 9, 1895; September 12, 1895.

Beaver County Democrat, July 12, 1894.

Claremore Progress, October 27, 1894.

Daily Oklahoman, June 5, 10 and 21, 1894; August 1, 1894; October 23, 25, and 27–28, 1894; November 1, 6, 11, 16, 23–24, 28 and 30, 1894; January 15–16 and 26, 1895; February 9, 1895; January 10, 1900; February 9, 1900.

Dallas News, January 25, 1895.

Edmond Sun-Democrat, October 25, 1894.

Eufaula *Indian Journal*, June 15 and 22, 1894; July 13, 1894; August 10, 1894; September 21, 1894; October 19, 1894; November 1-2 and 23, 1894; January 4, 18 and 25, 1895; March 1, 1895; April 5, 1895.

Fort Smith Elevator, June 1, 15 and 29, 1894; November 23, 1894; December 5, 1894; February 1, 1895; March 20 and 29, 1895; April 19, 1895; May 3, 1895; August 2, 1895; September 13, 1895; December 20, 1895.

Fort Smith *News-Record*, November 21, 1894; December 3, 1895.

Galveston Daily News, March 1, 1878.

Guthrie Daily Leader, July 21, 1894.

Kansas City Times, October 12, 1894.

Muskogee *Phoenix*, June 14 and 21, 1894; October 17, 1894; November 21, 1894; December 22, 1894; April 22, 1897.

Oklahoma Daily Press-Gazette, May 28–29, 1894; June 21, 1894.

Oklahoma Daily Star, December 28, 1894.

Oklahoma Daily Times-Journal, September 20, 1894; November 24, 1894; January 15, 1895; July 27, 1895; October 1, 1895; December 4, 1895.

Oklahoma State Capital, June 2 and 21, 1894; July 5–6, 1894; August 1 and 3-4, 1894; September 20, 1894; October 24–26, 1894; November 5 and 15, 1894; December 26 and 29, 1894; January 14–15, 19 and 22, 1895; February 9 and 14, 1895; March 29, 1895; July 13, 1895; September 21, 1895; January 28, 1898; February 7, 1900; March 3, 1900; May 19, 1903; June 25, 1903; August 1, 1903.

South McAlester Capital, October 11, 1894; November 1, 1894; April 4, 1895; September 5, 1895.

Stillwater *Eagle-Gazette*, July 19, 1894; October 11, 1894; November 1, 22 and 29, 1894; December 6, 1894; February 14, 1895.

Tahlequah *Cherokee Advocate*, June 6, 1894; October 10, 1894; January 10, 1895; February 13, 1895.

Vinita *Indian Chieftain*, August 9, 1894; October 11 and 25, 1894; January 24,

1895; February 14 and 28, 1895; April 4 and 25, 1895; May 2, 1895; July 18 and 25, 1895; August 1, 8 and 15, 1895; September 5, 1895; February 20, 1896; March 12 and 26, 1896; April 8 and 23, 1896.

Wichita Daily Eagle, July 20, 1894; November 22, 1894.

INTERVIEWS

In *Indian-Pioneer History,* Oklahoma Historical Society, Archives and Manuscript Division, Volumes 1–112.

         Byrd, William. Vol. 1, 482.

         Calhoun, James. Vol. 18, 128–29.

         Griffin, Frank I. Vol. 26, 439–40.

         Hill, Fielden Salyer. Vol. 29, 129.

         Humberd, John C. Vol. 5, 287.

         McDermott, Jess. Vol. 7, 14–15.

         Matheson, Alex R. Vol. 6, 435–36.

         Reynolds, John M. Vol. 41, 378–79.

         Ross, Elizabeth. Vol. 42, 489–90.

         Scott, J.W. Vol. 44, 19–21.

         Still, Amanda L. Vol. 10, 164.

         Surrell, Maude Brown. Vol. 87, 483–84.

         Taylor, Burl. Vol. 10, 315–16, 320.

         Taylor, William. Vol. 10, 349–52.

         Turley, James W. Vol. 11, 51–53.

         Warren, Clarence O. Vol. 11, 228–29, 232–33.

BOOKS

Croy, Homer. *He Hanged Them High.* New York: Duell, Sloan and Pearce; Boston: Little, Brown and Company, 1952.

Drago, Harry Sinclair. *Outlaws on Horseback.* New York: Dodd, Mead and Company, 1964.

Emery, J. Gladstone. *Court of the Damned.* New York: Comet Press Books, 1959.

Gideon, D.C. *Indian Territory: Descriptive, Bibliographical and Genealogical...With a General History of the Territory.* New York: The Lewis Publishing Company, 1901.

Glasscock, C.B. *Then Came Oil: The Story of the Last Frontier.* Indianapolis: Bobbs-Merrill Company, 1938.

Haley, J. Evetts. *Fort Concho and the Texas Frontier*. San Angelo, Texas: San Angelo *Standard-Times*, 1952.

Harkey, Dee. *Mean as Hell*. Albuquerque: University of New Mexico Press, 1948.

Harman, S.W. *Hell on the Border: He Hanged Eighty-Eight Men*. Fort Smith, Arkansas: The Phoenix Publishing Company, 1898.

Harrington, Fred Harvey. *Hanging Judge*. Caldwell, Idaho: The Caxton Printers, Ltd., 1951.

Hart, Herbert M. *Old Forts of the Southwest*. Seattle, Washington: Superior Publishing Company, 1964.

Katz, William Loren. *The Black West*. Garden City, New York: Doubleday and Company, Inc., 1971.

Leckie, William H. *The Buffalo Soldiers: A Narrative of the Negro Cavalry of the West*. Norman, Oklahoma: University of Oklahoma Press, 1967.

Rickey, Don, Jr. *Forty Miles a Day on Beans and Hay: The Enlisted Soldier Fighting the Indian Wars*. Norman, Oklahoma: University of Oklahoma Press, 1963.

Shinkle, James D. *Reminiscences of Roswell Pioneers*. Roswell, New Mexico: Hall-Poorbaugh Press, Inc., 1966.

Shirley, Glenn. *Henry Starr: Last of the Real Badmen*. New York: David McKay Company, Inc., 1965.

_____. *Law West of Fort Smith: A History of Frontier Justice in the Indian Territory, 1834–1896*. New York: Henry Holt and Company, 1957.

_____. *Toughest of Them All*. Albuquerque: University of New Mexico Press, 1953.

Stanley, Mack. *Hanging Judge and His Desperadoes*. Spiro, Oklahoma: n.p., 1983.

Stansbery, Lon R. *The Passing of 3-D Ranch*. Tulsa: n.p., 1913.

Sullivan, W.J.L. *Twelve Years in the Saddle for Law and Order on the Frontiers of Texas*. Austin: von Boeckman-Jones Company, Printers, 1909.

Teall, Kaye M. *Black History in Oklahoma*. Oklahoma City: Oklahoma City Public Schools, 1971.

Wellman, Paul I. *Dynasty of Western Outlaws*. Garden City, New York: Doubleday and Company, Inc., 1961.

ARTICLES

Berry, W.T. "How McDermott Was Robbed." Fort Smith *Times-Democrat*, November 6, 1894; Ardmore *State Herald*, November 22, 1894.

Bobo, L.B. "Reminiscences of Pioneer Days." *Chronicles of Oklahoma*, Vol. 23, No. 3, Autumn 1945.

Braun, Bill. "The Life and Hard Times of Crawford Goldsby." *True Frontier*, October 1974.

Breihan, Carl W. "Cherokee Bill Goldsby." *Real West*, January 1970; reprinted in *Oldtimers Wild West*, December 1978.

Bristow, George, as told to Olevia E. Myers. "I Helped Capture Cherokee Bill!" *Frontier Times*, June-July 1967.

_____. "Hectic-Days in Territory: In the Early Nineties." *The Ranchman*, October 1942.

Burkholder, Edwin V. "The Tragic Weakness of Cherokee Bill." *Male*, July 1958.

"Cherokee Bill." *Gunslingers of the West*, Winter 1966–67.

Cotton, Robert. "'Cherokee Bill' Was Among Most Bloodthirsty Outlaws." *Nowata Daily Star*, October 12, 1960.

Etter, Jim. "Cherokee Bill's Brother." *True West*, September-October 1974.

_____. "The Day Sequoyah Houston Fell to Cherokee Bill." *Frontier Times*, October-November 1972.

Gordon, Wes. "'Why Should I Use Fists to Fight? Guns Is Better': Cherokee Bill." *Man's Western*, August-September 1959.

Havelock-Bailie, Captain R. "Cherokee Bill's Last Stand." *True Western Adventures*, Spring 1958.

Lehman, M.P. "A Good Day for Dying." *Golden West*, May 1965; reprinted in *The West*, February 1972.

"Life Record of Cherokee Bill." *Fort Smith Municipal Police Journal* (annual), 1952.

McKennon, C.H. "The Scourge of the Territory." *Wildcat*, June 8, 1979.

Monan, Charles. "Unlucky 13." *Real West*, July 1960.

Penot, Barbara Hale. "The Hanging of Cherokee Bill." *True Frontier*, January 1969. Reprinted in *True Frontier*, Special Issue 1, 1971.

Stansbery, Lon R. "Cowtown Catoosa, 'Dark and Bloody Ground,' I.T." *Tulsa World*, July 27, 1937.

Stone, Arnold. "I Came to Die." *Real Adventure*, March 1957.

Turpin, Robert F. "Saga of the Deadly Cook Gang." *True Frontier*, November 1969; reprinted in *Best of the Badmen*. Sparta, Illinois: Majors Magazines, Inc., 1973.

Whitmire, Mrs. E.H. "A Short Sketch of the Life of Cherokee Bill." *Indian-Pioneer History*, Oklahoma Historical Society, Archives and Manuscript Division, Vol. 11, 378–82.

Winston, Morris. "A Murderer Is Loose on the Cherokee Strip." *Great West*, April 1967.

INDEX

173